POWER & PLEASURE

*The Devonshire House
Jubilee Ball 1897*

ELISABETH KEHOE

UNICORN

To Emily and Alice, the lights of my heart

Published in 2024 by Unicorn, an imprint of
Unicorn Publishing Group LLP
Charleston Studio,
Meadow Business Centre,
Ringmer,
Lewes BN8 5RW

www.unicornpublishing.org

Text © Elisabeth Kehoe
Images courtesy of National Portrait Gallery. Colourised by Matt Loughrey

ISBN 978-1-916846-27-2
10 9 8 7 6 5 4 3 2 1

Design: AH Design
Printed in Turkey by Finetone

CONTENTS

Lady Randolph Churchill, Winston Churchill's mother,
as the Empress Theodora, wife of Justinian

LIST OF LAFAYETTE STUDIO PORTRAITS

The Duchess of Devonshire
as Zenobia, Queen of Palmyra

I

INTRODUCTION

At midnight the first supper was served. The Prince of Wales, with the Duchess of Devonshire, led the procession. Down the staircase they went, into the garden, for it was there that supper was served, in a huge tent of blue and yellow canvas, with tapestry draping its walls. By a pretty conceit each table was around a palm tree, the trunk piercing its centre, the fronds waving above. From the branches hung electric lamps, throwing into brilliant light the rich embroidery of the costumes and the colours of the tapestry.[1]

O<small>N 2 J</small>ULY 1897 <small>THE</small> D<small>EVONSHIRE</small> H<small>OUSE</small> B<small>ALL WAS HOSTED BY THE</small> Duke and Duchess of Devonshire (*see page viii and page 3*) to honour Queen Victoria's sixty years on the throne: her Diamond Jubilee. The event was the most important social and political marker of this momentous celebration year, and inclusion in the event was a barometer of power and influence. By making the party a fancy-dress ball – with costumes selected from the period before the eighteenth century – the Duchess, the most significant political hostess of her day, cleverly transformed what was a political and diplomatic occasion into an evening of fun, artistic endeavour and creativity.

The event brings into focus the importance of such occasions in articulating and giving expression to the social and political rituals that provided a physical and psychical separation between those of high social and political status – aided and abetted by shared backgrounds, values and authority networks – and those further down the pyramid. What this fancy-dress party vividly demonstrates, too, is the inclusion of outsiders, traditionally excluded from such demonstrations of power. Because of changing economic conditions and global dynamics – including threats from other nations – and, significantly, the Prince of Wales's (*see page 9*) role in bringing in financially powerful friends, the British upper classes showed an adaptability and survival instinct by incorporating the outsider who proved useful.

The Devonshire House Ball provides a fascinating example of how skilled at retaining power the ruling elite had become, after centuries of erecting the highest barriers to entry to their privileged world. Even money had, hitherto, failed to open social doors to all but the very few. By 1897, however, the British aristocratic classes were increasingly permeable, as wealthy foreigners, manufacturers and plutocrats befriended the heir and his entourage. A reduction in traditional land incomes – on which their status had been based – and the entry of foreign and internal competition had provided opportunities for the upper classes to generate income by investing or marrying outside their usual spheres.

The guest list of the Ball provides interesting reading, as we shall see. The primary social event of the Jubilee was hosted by a foreigner. And as the long line of some 700 splendidly arrayed guests waited to climb the stairs, serenaded by the orchestra and surrounded by the magnificent scent of thousands of flowers, the Duchess could be reassured that she had succeeded: her party was the social triumph of the season, if not the century.

In 1897, Queen Victoria had reigned for an incredible sixty years over an island nation which now dominated Asia by governing India as well as large swathes of West and East Africa. Britain's navy was supreme, her wealth extraordinary, and the tendrils of political, economic and diplomatic power ran far and deep: indeed, two of Victoria's grandchildren became, or were married to, Europe's most powerful emperors. Unlike the Golden Jubilee celebrations of 1887, when all the crowned heads of Europe had gathered to celebrate, in 1897 there were so many political and diplomatic rifts in Europe that Joseph Chamberlain, the Colonial Secretary, proposed not to include them in the celebrations, but instead to use the Jubilee to demonstrate British imperial might by marching soldiers from all corners of the Empire through the streets of London. Furthermore, Victoria –

The Duke of Devonshire KG
as the Emperor Charles V

notoriously reluctant to open her well-stuffed purse – had refused to pay for any of the huge costs, which had to be met by the Treasury. One of the ways to economise was to conduct the event in the open air, and on 22 June the Queen, accompanied by 50,000 troops, was driven in the open state landau through streets lined with thousands of cheering spectators. They roared wildly, waved flags, and broke into renditions of the national anthem.

It was a magnificent display, designed for the people and for Her Majesty, who so seldom appeared in public. The emotional occasion – which gave Victoria enormous gratification, and which thrilled her subjects – was hardly a glamorous event for the social elite, however. The Queen was too stout and unfit to dismount from the carriage, so the thanksgiving service at St Paul's Cathedral was rather unexcitingly held on the cathedral steps while she remained sitting in her landau. The events that followed that week to mark the Jubilee were more ceremonial than glamorous: a reception in the Ball Room at Buckingham Palace to receive loyal addresses from both Houses of Parliament, for example, or a gathering of 10,000 schoolchildren to pay their respects at Paddington Station while loyal addresses from the London School Board were made, and a reception at Slough where children from the British Orphan Society presented the Queen with a bouquet.

With the exception of a garden party at the end of the week for those foreign dignitaries who had come to London despite having no official part to play, there was little to satisfy the appetite of the European royalties and British aristocracy who wanted to dress in their finery and flaunt their jewels. The glittering climax of the celebrations was therefore to be the Devonshire House Ball. Only 700 guests were to be included. This was intended to keep the Ball extraordinarily select, and also to avoid past fiascos of other hapless hosts whose London events had been so crowded that the Prince of Wales had walked out.

Although it was out of the question that Victoria would herself attend, she did not disapprove of such entertainments. Elaborate costume balls had featured throughout her reign before Albert's death, beginning with the Eglinton Tournament, which had included a medieval joust. And the Queen and Prince Albert had given a number of fancy-dress parties, in 1842, 1845 and 1851 – and the tradition had been continued by Bertie and Alexandra, who presided over the famous Marlborough House Ball of 1874.

The 700 guests had had weeks to prepare what was inevitably a strong sartorial statement. Some individuals decided to create a costume that would remain secret; others joined a group linked by a common theme. Although the invitations were officially sent out only one month in advance, there were many guests who knew beforehand that they would be included – which gave them time to choose their friends, and to coordinate and order their hand-made costumes.

There were five courts presented, led by Ladies Londonderry, Tweedmouth, Warwick and Ormonde, as well as an 'Oriental' one presided over by the Duchess herself. An Italian procession and a grouping of allegorical costumes were also planned. It was not necessarily a sign of social Siberia not to be included in one of the groups. The costumes were used to send all kinds of signals: some guests, such as the Duke of Somerset, (*see page 165*) chose to come as a very illustrious ancestor. Jennie Churchill (*see page vi*) remarked: 'Where so many magnificent and exquisite dresses were worn it is invidious to mention names, but I remember thinking that the Duchess of Somerset's (*see page 167*) was the most correct and beautiful, with every detail perfectly carried out, the result being absolutely perfect.'[2] The very wealthy spent a king's ransom on magnificent clothing, which they then smothered in costly jewels. It was not a night for subtlety or tact. Older women dressed as young ingénues and young women wore the scantiest of outfits, under the guise of the historical accuracy of representing, say, a Greek goddess clad in little more than the filmiest of drapery.

It was a night to show off, a night to outdo one other, and one to settle old scores. There had been a scramble to secure the services of the best costumiers and dressmakers in London and even in Paris – and there were reports that in this endeavour the gentlemen had left the ladies in the shade, such was their eagerness to compete. The Duke of Marlborough (*see page 93*), for example, had demanded the services of Worth in Paris and had – to the couturier's awe – insisted on a Louis XVI costume that had cost a shocking FF 5,000 (nearly £20,000 today).

II
HISTORICAL BACKGROUND

DOMINANCE

A T THE TIME OF QUEEN VICTORIA'S DIAMOND JUBILEE, BRITAIN WAS IN a dominating global position, largely due to her extensive Empire. With the strongest navy in the world, the nation vigorously protected vital trade routes and ports, relying on successful imports and exports to further develop and sustain a huge economy. In 1897, territories under British mandate, control or influence covered close to 14 million square miles – about a quarter of the planet's land mass – and the Queen could claim to reign over 450 million people, approximately one-quarter of the world's entire population. It was an extraordinarily ambitious undertaking, and the Empire had grown organically, through military, commercial and cultural dominance, resulting in a loosely bound conglomerate that looked undefeatable.

A successful industrial revolution had underpinned this dominance, all but making the nation appear overwhelmingly pre-eminent and impregnable. This was untrue. There were many competitors keen to attack and replace British interests, and growing economies such as the former colony of the United States, as well as Germany, France, Russia and Japan, were snapping at Britain's heels. In addition to external threats, the nation was facing a series of internal changes that had the potential to bring about profound upheavals and challenges to the hegemonic social, cultural, political and financial structure upon which the monarchy relied.

One of the greatest strengths of the Empire was its stable monarchical structure, with a dutiful Queen and a reliable aristocracy. In order to preserve this stability, however, the elite status of the nobility and landed gentry had to be sustained in order for them to fulfil their political and economic obligations. The aristocracy of Britain had traditionally relied on income from their lands to generate their high incomes. From the 1870s, however, the capital value of the land started to drop as the income lessened that it could generate. A series of poor harvests and rising import and export competition contributed to this. Rents chargeable for land that was less profitable dropped, as tenants were faced with cheaper imports available thanks to improved shipping times from, notably, America and Australia. As the tenants could not afford to pay their landlords the rents they had previously received, so the incomes of the landowners fell, and their dominant status was at risk.

By 1897, the elite had had time to adjust. Some chose to retrench, others sold off their lands – bit by bit – thus losing their source of income and merely staving off inevitable decline. Others, more fortunate, were able to use their property, if well situated, for railways, factories and other developments. Still others were fortunate enough to be sitting on mining and other assets. A further source of income generation was to marry money. Once frowned upon, marriage to wealthy foreigners – mainly American heiresses – became gradually accepted, especially after the marriage of Jennie Jerome, daughter of a New York speculator, to Lord Randolph Churchill in 1874. Jennie's close friendship – and later, liaison – with the Prince of Wales opened the social doors for a series of American brides to join the highest echelons of society.

Jennie, her sister Leonie Leslie, Minnie Paget (*see page 99*), Consuelo Vanderbilt (Duchess of Marlborough), Mary Endicott Chamberlain, Mary (known as May) Goelet, the singer Fanny Ronalds, Natica Yznaga (Lady Lister Kaye) and Consuelo Yznaga (Lady Manchester, daughter-in-law of the Duchess of Devonshire (*see page 163*)) were but some of the American guests at the Ball. The heiress daughter of a New York war profiteer, May Goelet (later Duchess of Roxburghe) made an especially stunning impact, dressed as Scheherazade, her costume tailored in Paris from drapes of gauze, belted at her tiny waist, and elaborated with multitudes of gems. Her jewelled headdress held a gem draped on her forehead, to great effect – as was the billowing feather that topped the tiara.

THE POOR ARE ALWAYS WITH US

THE JUBILEE, HOWEVER CELEBRATORY, did not take place in isolation and the context of the late Victorian period was noted for a growing awareness of poverty in the lowest socio-economic groups. Sensational publications, such as the Rev. Andrew Mearn's *The Bitter Cry of Outcast London*, published in 1883, and William Booth of the Salvation Army's *In Darkest England and the Way Out* – published in seventeen volumes, 1889–1902 – gave some inkling of society's deep-set problems. Concerns about social welfare and structural societal inequality had been articulated throughout the century, from Malthus to Henry Mayhew, Charles Dickens and Baroness Burdett-Coutts through to 'the Christian Socialists in the 1840s and 1850s, to Canon Barnett, Octavia Hill and the Charity Organisation Society of 1869'.[3]

These voices had grown in volume and, by the turn of the century, such concerns had translated to more intense preoccupation about social ills and possible economic solutions, and to concrete calls for action. The rumblings announcing the resumption in 1899 of the Boer conflict in South Africa, for example, highlighted the general unfitness of the troops because of poor living standards. An 'Interdepartmental Committee on Physical Deterioration' reported in 1904 that Sir Frederick Maurice's 'complaints of the unfitness of many army recruits in the Boer War, amply confirmed the poor food, overcrowded housing and terrible living conditions'.[4] Christian and other reformers were both vocal and active in establishing charitable endeavours and also in pushing for reform.

The Great Dock Strike of 1889, when the dockers demanded the 'docker's tanner' of 6d. an hour, saw the emergence of three powerful leaders, John Burns, Tom Mann and Benjamin Tillet. The strikers gained a milestone victory, as 100,000 workers won their pay claim. The action formed an important step in the development of the British labour movement, establishing strong trade unions. The strike elicited great public sympathy and media engagement. It came soon after the equally famous match-girls' action at the Bryant & May factory, where fourteen-hour workdays, appalling conditions and poor pay caused a major outcry.

HRH The Prince of Wales as Grand Prior of the
Order of St John of Jerusalem

Following the strike's success, a union was formed, and in 1901 the factory ceased using white phosphorus, which had caused so many health problems to its workers.

Both the Liberals and Conservatives believed in social reform, but what differed was the ways in which to achieve it, to what extent and at what cost. There was not, on either side of the House, a desire for rapid and systemic change, which came in the wake of the Radical and Labour movements. Incremental measures and laws were preferred, such as the Immigration Act of 1891, which followed on from the Elementary Education Act of 1870, by making elementary education not only compulsory but free. In 1893 the school leaving-age was raised to eleven years. Overall, a growing middle class benefited from better living conditions – but the ills of poverty remained.

Politicians and social commentators alike found it incumbent upon them to examine the causes for social distress. Population shifts accounted for increasing uncertainties and the ever-present possibility of class conflict. Between 1850 and 1920, huge migration (some 45 million people) took place from the Old World to the New. This massive population shift had huge implications for the growing societies of the Americas, of course, but this 'mass exodus' also brought in its wake change in Europe, 'reducing the size of the workforce, thereby driving up wages and offering further rewards for innovation, mechanisation and industrialisation'.[5] The accommodation made to engage with this changing landscape affected all socio-economic groups of English society, and the ever-present need to avoid profound social unrest. Revolutionary movements in continental Europe – with 1848 a crisis year – provoked great fear in Britain.

So, despite outward stability, there were markers of potential trouble for a nation in which many were excluded from the economic engagement that makes for a settled populace. Property tenancy was unavailable to the poor and the very poor. The rapid rise in population from the 1840s and concomitant drive from countryside to towns exacerbated the issues. The Poor Law (Amendment) Act of 1834 had been deliberately designed to make poverty so dreadful that it would be seen as a situation to be avoided at all costs. Workhouses were specifically designed to make life more unpleasant than being outside. The continuation of this policy was one of the reasons for the rise of Chartism, which was the first mass movement driven by the working classes. It originated in 1836 in London, following the failure of the 1832 Reform Act to extend enfranchisement beyond those who owned property.

The shift in work patterns also meant that more people were engaged in the service industries, usually concentrated in the towns and cities. Many worked in manufacturing, mining, trade and retail. As the middle class grew as a sector, the demand for domestic servants rose. In the past, only the very wealthiest could afford paid help. By the end of the nineteenth century, however, there were 1.5 million domestic servants, representing 4 per cent of the population. Butlers, footmen, cooks, housekeepers, maids, valets and scullery maids provided hours of cheap labour, and complaints about finding and keeping such help were rife. 'Like the rain and the poor, the "servant question" is ever with us,' lamented a newspaper in 1899.[6]

These concerns gave way to lively and critical debate. A thoughtful employer shared that she had 'learned to treat my servants like human beings', and indeed, suggested that 'The Servant Question' might more appropriately 'be labelled the "Mistress Question"'.[7] This questioning might have been primarily a middle-class preoccupation, but landed estates and town houses also faced rising competition for affordable high-quality workers, many of whom were better educated and more knowledgeable about their rights.

TRADE LAWS

Although Chartism had ultimately failed by 1850, its development was a signpost of trouble to come for the elite classes. A further worry to the aristocracy and the settled order was the repeal of the Corn Laws. These protectionist measures had been in place from 1815 to 1846, a series of tariffs on imported cereal grains – corn, wheat, oats and barley – legislated in order to protect domestic producers. The laws had been introduced by

Parliament to protect the landlord interest during the depression following the Napoleonic Wars (1803–15). Even when food supplies were short, causing great suffering, there was either a ban or a high tariff imposed on imports.

These measures favoured those who owned land, and they incited significant opposition, especially after the Great Famine in Ireland of 1845–52. The repeal of the Corn Laws, when it finally happened, benefited the vast majority of the population, while reducing the income at the very top. In addition to causing huge financial hardship, the protectionist laws, its opponents successfully demonstrated, had harmed economic development – both production and trade. It has been convincingly argued that the Repeal of the Corn Laws and the 1832 Reform Act resulted in the 'growth and advance of the middle classes and their power'.[8]

SHIFTS IN POWER

By the year 1897, we can observe that there had been some shifts in how the financial and commercial power of Britain was concentrated. There were principally three rival groups. The relative influence of each group was changing over time – reflected in majorities in Parliament, by legislative reforms (there were fifteen Acts of Parliament passed between 1833 and 1878 just to deal with various trades).

The first group, the landed elite, had its traditional bastion of dominance based on land ownership. As land values began decreasing in the 1870s, this elite fought to overcome the interests of the second group, the commercial-based London elite. The northern manufacturing elite was another separate group, who were more than capable of fighting for their own interests.[9]

The revenues from land from the 1870s had been, as noted above, on a downward trend. What is often called 'the Great Depression' in agriculture reduced rental revenue from arable lands, which reduced land values. Although these conditions were challenging, other areas of the economy went some way to picking up the slack. Britain had the reputation as 'workshop of the world' – as exemplified by the hugely successful Great

Exhibition in 1851 — and the British economy grew in other areas as well. There was a large increase in the 'professions' such as the clergy, medical staff, lawyers, and those working in finance and in the growing service economy. By the late 1890s, it has been convincingly argued, it became clear that Britain's was a commercial, or commercial/financial economy, rather than an industrial one.[10] The importance of trade within such an economic landscape was obvious to the political class, and the arguments surrounding it were to do with protectionism — the case for and against.

The decisive electoral success of the Liberals in November 1885 placed free trade — a laissez-faire capitalism as espoused by the powerful and magisterial Prime Minister Gladstone, who favoured no tariffs and minimal intervention in the economy — at the centre of British politics. The barriers that had helped agricultural producers were abandoned in favour of the City of London: the financiers and banking infrastructure, and, ultimately, the new asset-owning elite.

For many, life did not improve. Radical politicians appealed to those who recognised that structural change was needed. It was a complex economic picture: Britain was still a strong, high-performing nation, but there were challenges and it is important to recognise that within a world of overall economic success, the bulk of Londoners 'still lived in near-poverty'. Although the 'average working wage' for 1900 was usually given as £1.15s., cookery books for the working class generally assume that families lived on about £1.10s. a week — 'of which something like a quarter would go to pay the rent'.[11]

Thus the potentially problematic nature of the overt display of wealth portrayed by the Jubilee parties generally, and the flamboyant Ball specifically, had to be translated into a kind of social good, a public proclamation of the enduring commitment by the ruling elite to the overall wellbeing of the nation. The powerful at play had to be seen as playing for Britain, for her continued global success as a mighty economic powerhouse. Politicians and other members of the social elite would be invited to join in the celebrations like the Ball. And such was the draw of the Devonshires, along with the royal cachet of the Prince of Wales, it was so much of a social disgrace to be excluded from the ultimate festival of festivities, that many of those humiliated by the lack of an invitation chose to be away from London.

A CASE FOR UNITY

CELEBRATIONS OF VICTORIA'S DIAMOND JUBILEE were an opportunity to proclaim once again – as the Golden Jubilee had done so magnificently a decade before – the overwhelming power and prestige of Britain on the global stage. The message was destined for three audiences: first, the people at home. The nation's governing elite set great store by the virtue of democracy – and thus the ruled needed to be reassured that all was well and as it should be, and that their best interests were being served by their leaders. For many, the spectacle provided by delegations and deputations from all the colonies, dependencies and dominions was the first time they had experienced the full extent of the Empire. As one commentator later wrote: 'Not even Rome in her proudest days could ever show such an assemblage of Emperors, Kings, Princes and Potentates – European, Indian, African – as were included in that memorable procession.'[12]

Secondly, a grand show was necessary to convince the colonial leaders that the mother country had the will and the resource to protect and increase their prosperity, and to deliver untold advantages to her colonies. A massive naval and armed forces display would reinforce the critical message that remaining under British rule and influence was the surest bet to achieving trade and prosperity. A further demonstration of the advantages of being within this extraordinary national and global network would be experienced by the award of medals and honours, within the magnificent framework of pageantry, ceremony and royal flair that the British had perfected.

Lastly, a significant display of raw power could speak a thousand words. For the visiting dignitaries from rival nations such as France, Germany, Japan and the USA, among others, let alone the thousands of Americans

From left to right: *Mrs Grenfell as Marie de Medici; The Rt. Hon. Sir W.V. Harcourt MP as Simon Lord Harcourt, Lord Chancellor 1710; The Rt Hon. A.J. Balfour MP as a gentleman of Holland*

and colonial visitors who poured into the capital to join the celebrations, this was a theatrical bonanza, complete with royal splendour, dazzling uniforms and frocks, sparkling jewels, fireworks, parades, pageants, floral decorations, music, illuminations and entertainments.

In this set-piece, everyone had a role to play. This is where the duties and responsibilities of the royal family became evident, as did those of the governing elite. In 1897, the upper crust – perhaps 10,000 people – held and deployed status, power and influence. The aristocracy and wealthy gentry thus had a vested interest in maintaining the status quo, one that favoured the accident of birth above everything else, and one that enabled the wealthy to continue to accrue riches. There were, admittedly, some clever and hardworking individuals who had managed to become rich or to achieve feats of recognised prowess, but historically this had very, very rarely admitted them to the innermost sanctum of privilege.

Aristocrats such as the Duke and Duchess of Devonshire were expected, along with other members of the nobility, to do their bit, and to do it handsomely. Even within high society, there were different sets, and one of the arts of great hosting was to know how to accommodate these overlapping and at times conflicting groups. To be a member of the privileged upper set was to be – by nothing more than an accident of birth – privileged and wealthy, with an expectation to enjoy a life full of pleasure. However, there was also a clear expectation, for both men and women – albeit in very different roles – to be active participants in the nation's political life.

The business of government, therefore, played a significant part in the lives of those members of the most elite social circles, and it is in this role that most of the overlaps of the various sets took place. The old-fashioned, wealthy territorial grandees – led by the Duke of Devonshire – wielded the most traditional political power, both locally and nationally. The prospect, though, begun by the Liberal leader Gladstone in 1882, of granting some form of limited independence – in the form of Home Rule – to Ireland, created deep and bitter divisions between friends, allies and even families. Gladstone's ministry fell briefly in 1885 because of the cataclysmic results of this divisiveness.

Home Rule for Ireland was one of the most important issues of the day, and was a constant thorn in the premier's side. The island had a long history of aggressive conquest, with inhabitants in the same localities who espoused differing alliances and religious views. Sectarian divisions were exacerbated by the class divide: Protestants – many of them of English and Scottish origin – were the dominant land-owning class and the lack of a coherent and fair land redistribution policy was a source of constant unrest and indeed rebellion. Irish leaders achieved limited success but the arrival on the scene in the 1880s of the Protestant landlord Charles Stewart Parnell announced a new era in bitter Anglo-Irish politics. In addition to promoting sedition at home and bombings and violence in England, Irish rebels were led with political astuteness by Parnell, who drove an agenda of reform that Gladstone found reasonable and inevitable.

Gladstone felt that the need for discussion and some limited form of independence for Ireland was essential for any kind of peace. Others vehemently disagreed. The repercussions of this divisiveness ran very deep. The Duke of Devonshire had reason for his hostility to independence for Ireland, after the murder of his brother Lord Frederick Cavendish in May 1882. Cavendish, newly appointed Chief Secretary for Ireland, was killed hours after his arrival in Dublin, along with the Permanent Under-Secretary Thomas Henry Burke, in what became known as the Phoenix Park killings. The assassination was performed by a militant nationalist splinter group, the Invincibles. The killings were brutal; weapons used were scalpels and surgical blades, and the men were stabbed multiple times. The outcry was immediate, and resulted in even more toughening of laws to repress and inhibit Irish struggles for land reform and some form of independence.

These murders had the further consequence of alienating the Duke from ever adopting any kind of a sympathetic position on legitimate aspirations – in Ireland and in England – for much-needed reforms. It also alienated the Duke from political colleagues, especially on the Liberal bench, who wished throughout the 1880s to see some forward movement on a resolution to the violence. Devonshire no longer felt comfortable with Gladstone and other colleagues, for example, who wished to engage in constructive debate with

Parnell. He was much happier with the Conservatives, whose position was far more intransigent. The Tory creation of, and support for, Ulster had ramifications that are still being acted out today, and have caused multiple miseries and tragedy over the decades.

The profound disagreement over Ireland was one barrier that, to the Duke, was inflexible. There were no Irish sympathisers welcome at Devonshire House. Hartington expected his friends to follow his lead. There was an elasticity in the interpretation of what was meant by high society, but there was absolutely no room for perceived disloyalty to the Crown or to the Empire. Sympathisers to Ireland's plight were very much cast in the mould of traitors to imperial values, and were totally unwelcome.

Traditional old families, such as those of Cecil, Cavendish, Churchill or Balfour, were now expected to associate with men of new position, such as Asquith, Chamberlain, Gorst or Haldane 'in society drawing rooms as well as in the House'. They were expected to entertain and to be entertained by Rothschilds and Sassoons at country homes, as the country house weekend format formerly reserved to the old aristocracy and highest county set was no longer merely the preserve of the old elite: politicians 'of varied origin' were now increasingly accommodated at country houses where political and social life intertwined.[13] An adherence to the imperial status quo could never be at question, however. Outsiders could be accepted, but only if they adhered strictly to the prevailing cultural, social and political code of the ruling elite.

This transition was difficult for some. Socialite (and, later in life, socialist) Frances, Countess of Warwick (known as Daisy), recalled 'the amazement' at a famous country house when the Duke of Devonshire 'announced at luncheon that he was expecting Mr Joseph Chamberlain for the weekend'. There was shock as the company realised that 'the radical from Birmingham' was 'to storm the ducal door!' Daisy remembered that someone in the party had asked her if she thought Chamberlain 'would know how to conduct himself with outward decency'. A fellow guest had 'prophesied gloomily that he would eat peas with his knife, since anything was possible to a demagogue'.[14]

CHANGES AT THE TOP

As SOCIAL LIFE AT THIS HIGHEST LEVEL WAS ENTIRELY enmeshed with political life, it was clear that outsiders such as Chamberlain would have to be welcomed to the top tables. Some observers were unhappy, feeling that national life – and especially London life – was becoming more overtly ostentatious with the arrival of new talent and especially of money. After dining at Bath House, Piccadilly, with the millionaire Sir Julius Wernher and 'a company of financial magnates and their hangers-on', the social commentator Beatrice Webb acidly claimed: 'There might just as well have been a Goddess of Gold erected for overt worship – the impression of worship in thought, feeling and action could hardly have been stronger.'[15] Still, these new millionaires – Wernher's fortune heralded from South African diamonds – were 'eager to adopt the outward conventions of the old aristocracy'.[16] They looked to the older established nobility and entourage to mimic elitist behaviours.

The arrival and impact of new money was inescapable and undeniable. Of the thirty-one millionaires at the end of the nineteenth century, an astounding twenty-four were Jewish.[17] When the Rothschilds crossed over to the Conservatives, a formidable alliance of Tory rule and Jewish money combined to a 'domination of certain social strata, particularly that of the super-rich merchant class'.[18] There were big shifts in a hitherto familiar political and social landscape, and these changes, accelerated by Bertie's determination to usher in his rich mates, brought about a certain unfamiliar fluidity in what had been a very static social order.

Such fluidity was reflected, too, in the all-important process of presentations at court. The numbers increased substantively, and further drawing rooms were added to accommodate Victoria's reception of the young debutantes.[19] Americans and daughters of plutocrats were, controversially for many, introduced to this highest echelon of society. The traditional barriers to entry of birth and long-term historical ownership of landed estates were being dramatically and permanently broken year by year – by 1891 fewer than half of the women presented were from the traditional background of yore, compared to 90 per cent in 1841.[20]

The Prince of Wales played a significant role in this redistribution of social cachet. His craving for amusement and diversion led to a seeking out of rich companions willing to play along with what was known as the Marlborough House set. Traditionalists were horrified by the low moral standards and addictions to high living and gambling, but court life with a dour Victoria left much to be desired. For the first time, the hegemonic domination of one social set, led by the court, became fractured. Influx of new capital from America and parts of the Empire, including South Africa and India, was accompanied by different manners and alternative ways of enjoying life – much of it far more ostentatious and glamorous than that of the landed classes, who still favoured country pursuits and restricted social gatherings in London during the season.

VICTORIA, ALBERT AND BERTIE

WHEN VICTORIA ASCENDED THE THRONE IN 1837, at the age of eighteen, she had high hopes of making a happy marriage. Unlike many royal alliances, her choice of partner, her first cousin, the German Prince Albert of Saxe-Coburg and Gotha, was made for love. She had initially disapproved of the possibility of the match when it was first mooted. But when she met Albert for the first time, she fell in love, later recording: 'It was with some emotion that I beheld Albert – who is *beautiful*.'[21] Although he had very little money, Albert brought more than good looks (Victoria, short and fat with buck teeth, was certainly no beauty) to the partnership: he had a love of the arts, intellectual pursuits and an indefatigable energy for good works and improving the life of his adopted country.

The couple were affectionate and Victoria was physically passionate. After their wedding in 1840, they went on to have nine children, despite the Queen's deep dislike of pregnancy. In fact, she notoriously disliked anything that kept her away from her beloved Albert, but not enough to abandon the marital bed. She especially disliked being pregnant, because it enabled her power-hungry spouse to take over more royal responsibilities.

Monsieur N. Boulatzell as Prince of Mingrelia

Even though Victoria was deeply in love with her handsome husband, they often fought over how much he could take on, from financial independence to outright involvements in government. Later, after his death, Victoria chose to forget, or gloss over, these differences, but the rows were both real and often ferocious. Both parties soon perfected the art of a good sulk.

It was not, perhaps, the most congenial environment for children, who arrived soon and in rapid succession. Their first child, Vicky, was born late in 1840 and a son, Albert Edward (known as Bertie), followed in 1841. From his early years, his parents found their heir challenging. He was not idle or mediocre, but he was under a huge amount of pressure, with very little fun in his life. With a lively, engaging personality, he soon rebelled against the interminable studies and strict rules imposed by his parents, tutors and teachers. As a youth, he gained, to his mother's despair, a well-deserved reputation as a playboy, known for a love of gambling, parties and womanising. His parents were stressed and concerned about him, but the situation was complex: there was a distinct preference for the clever, pretty Vicky and a competition between father and son. When Victoria chose to elevate her foreign spouse to the rank of Prince Consort in 1857, it gave him precedence over his son and heir; not an easy state of affairs.

Bertie gave his parents cause for concern, as he continued supervised study, travels and then a sojourn at Cambridge. Albert, who suffered increasingly ill health, and frequent gastric trouble, wrote to him frequently, especially after Bertie became involved in at least one liaison. After a visit to Cambridge in filthy weather, Albert returned home and became very ill. He never recovered. Suffering from depression, an inflated worry over his son and probably loneliness as a foreigner in England, he died two weeks later, in 1861, possibly of typhoid. Victoria was inconsolable, and Bertie was present at the deathbed only by chance, although his mother at first thanked him for his support.

However, such was the extent of her shock and misery that Victoria needed to lash out, and to find a scapegoat. This was easily found in the form of her unsatisfactory son, who had caused his father such heartache and worry. Her doctors, in the face of her intransigence and anger, did nothing to dissuade her of this view. Thenceforth, she chose to blame Bertie and to live in a state of perpetual semi-mourning and retirement; not choosing, nevertheless, to devolve political responsibility to her eldest son.

She continued to dislike, and disapprove of, her heir apparent, and she stubbornly refused – despite pleas from ministers and other parties – to allow the Prince any responsibilities of state beyond the absolute minimum. This intelligent, cheerful man, endowed with considerable charm (to which his mother remained immune), spent most of his time engaged in frivolous pursuits. Even admirers of the Queen and her dedication to duty observed that as 'he was not allowed to take part in the affairs of the country', she had 'herself left him with no alternative'.[22]

There were thus challenges posed by an uneasy monarchical situation after Prince Albert's premature death, and a simmering conflict between the Queen and the heir. Bertie's satisfactory marriage to the stunningly beautiful and elegant Princess Alexandra of Denmark (Alix) in 1863 went a little way to softening the Queen, as did the rapid arrival of grandchildren. The Prince was eager to celebrate his mother and to take responsibility for organising the Jubilee festivities. He, along with the government, felt that it was important to show the world that Britain was a strong economic force, and that despite the Queen's notorious reclusiveness, the monarchy was alive and well, and the succession secure. A strong monarchy was key to a strong Empire, and to a strong society.

The Prince established a committee to organise his mother's Diamond Jubilee ceremony at St Paul's, and asked the courtier politician Reginald Brett (later 2nd Viscount Esher) to join in his capacity of Permanent Secretary of the Office of Works. The group would take responsibility for the celebrations, including the service to be held outside St Paul's Cathedral. It was a prestigious committee: other members were the Archbishop of Canterbury, the Bishop of London, the Dean of St Paul's and the Duke of Portland as President. Bertie took the task very seriously; he loved becoming engaged in minute details. He insisted on being consulted on such matters as the siting of the stands for the children on Constitution Hill and the siting of seats for notables. Considerable attention was paid to the placement of

Victoria's controversial favourite, the Indian servant the Munshi, and his friends.

Celebrations included a reception in a large marquee in the garden at Buckingham Palace for the entourages of visiting dignitaries (no accommodation had been made for the stifling temperatures and after several guests had fainted, Brett ripped holes in the tent with his ceremonial rapier).[23] That night, a massive torchlit military tattoo was held in front of the Palace. An astounding 40,000 soldiers had attended the day. Brett and his wife were invited to the Ball, which he attended as, he declared, 'a gentleman of France of the year 1628 in which I suppose I shall look as big a tom fool as everybody else'.[24]

Bertie also set up a committee that included many of his Jewish friends, and these rich friends made substantial financial contributions to some of the celebrations. Members of the committee included Lord Rothschild, the Chief Rabbi, the wealthy Julius Wernher and Ernest Cassel (*see page 141*), as well as the Bishop of London. At the Prince's instigation, a fund was set up, and the Prince then asked his financier friends in the City of London to contribute generously. Such was the success of this endowment fund that one outcome was the King Edward's Hospital Fund, which still exists today as the King's Fund and is considered one of Edward's greatest legacies.[25]

HIGH SOCIETY

'THERE IS NO SUCH THING AS SOCIETY,' famously declared Britain's Conservative Prime Minister Margaret Thatcher in 1987. 'Society' in 1897, however, was beyond doubt the powerful engine driving the phenomenally successful enterprise that was Great Britain the Business State. Without society – specifically, high society – Britain was a small island, albeit a financial giant. With a superlative navy and resplendent army, Britain had sustained her predominant position as the world's greatest trader by ruthlessly seizing and dominating vast amounts of territory throughout the world and exploiting the resources. An industrial revolution, legislative and social reforms that encouraged private enterprise, and individual initiative had successfully underpinned a stable – if vulnerable – social structure that was propitious for wealth creation.

Power and prosperity on such a vast scale were achieved, as noted, largely by the determined expansion of Empire – through territory, influence and trade – and a domestic stability rigorously upheld. Troublemakers were exported, colonies repressed and the promotion of the values of free trade – spiritual as well as commercial – ruthlessly applied. 'Like almost everything else in nineteenth-century Britain, counter-revolutionary policy had an imperial dimension. Britain protected itself against upheaval by adopting policies that pacified home populations but heightened tensions on the imperial periphery.'[26]

Britain transported potential troublemakers to Australia and the Cape Colony. The government abandoned the sugar tariffs that protected colonial planters in Jamaica and British Guyana from foreign competition. This kept domestic prices low, and, for a population that was becoming more and more urban – by the turn of the century over three-quarters of England's inhabitants lived in sprawling towns and cities – that was crucial. Concomitantly, there had developed a culture dominated by getting and spending. The repeal of the Corn Laws in 1846 had, it bears repeating, been a transformative watershed that propelled Britain into a free market, one where commercialism became the ultimate driving force.

BROADENING THE FRANCHISE

UNLIKE REVOLUTIONARY FERMENTS ON THE CONTINENT[27] – so disruptive of economic prosperity – Britain had managed to quieten radical leanings by incorporating them into the body politic. Concerns about the potential for revolutionary activity were never far away from the political mind after the French Revolution and the mid-century unrest on the continent. The East End of London was often considered to be a hot bed of dissent, on the brink of rioting and other social unrest. The mid-1880s had witnessed disruption on a large scale as the economic conditions worsened for the miserable lower classes, trapped in poverty and squalid living conditions. There was therefore a consciousness in government of the need to maintain the momentum of improved incomes for the poorest in society, and for the disparities of wealth to be neutralised.

The reforms thus had as one objective to bring people into the political process in a meaningful way. As has been observed, after the broadening of the franchise – and the redistribution of constituencies in 1885 – 'the working classes were not only the objects of policy: to an unprecedented extent, they were active subjects within the political contest'. Because of this newfound importance, voters found themselves 'addressed as part of the nation more insistently than ever before'. The two major parties, although 'still dominated by holders of landed, rentier and industrial wealth', made efforts to widen their appeal to those closer to the bottom of the pyramid. Joseph Chamberlain, the Colonial Secretary bent on invigorating the Empire, was typically Conservative in his ambitions to build 'a race capable of sustaining and defending the empire, [that] were, in part, attempts to integrate the enfranchised working classes into the political system'.[28]

The Empire also had the hugely important role of providing employment – unemployment had fuelled much of the social unrest – in both import and export markets. Keeping the bulk of the population in work was a critical objective of any government in power, and the Jubilee provided an opportunity to demonstrate to the colonial leaders as well as to the foreign dignitaries and royalties that Britain was very much open for business. Many senior leaders were able to see the Devonshire House Ball as a commercial venture, one in which the best of the nation was to display her powers.

What followed the triumphant celebrations of Britain's Empire in June 1897, when Victoria marked her remarkable sixty years on the throne as both Queen of Great Britain and Empress of India, shows us that this event probably represented the zenith of the nation's power. The elderly monarch's territories stretched far and wide, encompassing the most extensive empire ever known, but, even before the first skirmishes of the Boer War, there were undercurrents of trouble. Aristocrats, by and large, still dominated

Lady Wolverton as Britannia

Britain's social, political and economic landscape, but the 'aristocratic ideal' of high-minded service and religious belief was gradually eroding.

As the nation's economy boomed and bust through the second half of the nineteenth century, legislative and social reforms increasingly had to reflect that the entrenchment and consolidation of Britain as a free-trading economy was being replaced by an increasingly internationalist and often chauvinistic mindset. And the mid-Victorian liberalism that had promoted self-reliance, buttressed by voluntary and co-operative societies and charitable benevolence, was gradually being replaced. Authors such as Dickens and journalists such as W.T. Stead had awakened awareness of the dire conditions in which Britain's poorest scraped together a miserable existence. Men and women from all walks of life were increasingly called upon to reach out to those less fortunate – this led to social reforms and to the growth of charitable ventures.

But, as Darwin's views on evolution gained credence after 1859, a competing argument, prioritising the view that progress – individual, national, and global – could only be achieved by providing an autonomous and self-regulating economy, also took hold. This rationale espoused strength as its credo: a strong Britain was a force for good in the world, just as strong individuals were the ones to be rewarded for their hard work. The 'undeserving poor' were to be prodded into performing, not helped to continue a life that was a drag on society.

To add to the troublesome undercurrents of some uncertainties and doubt, the traditional dominance of the Liberal party, favoured by the aristocratic landowners, was increasingly jeopardised by the Tories (Conservatives), who under the gifted leadership of Disraeli began winning elections; by 1881 they were the predominant party. Seen as the party of empire and patriotism, they enacted reforms that widened enfranchisement, but their commitment to free trade and commercialism meant that the revolutionary movements so destabilising on the continent were attenuated and muted in Britain. Social stability as an essential plank of widespread prosperity for all who worked hard was widely accepted as a reason to support the status quo, regardless of its inherent injustices of the privilege of birth.

In the search for, and maintenance of, this stability, two ideals stood relatively unchallenged. The first was the devotion by all classes to the royal family. The second was the pride taken in the British Empire. Disraeli – intending to flatter – had very cleverly consolidated the overlap between these two: Victoria loved being Empress of India and the extraordinary development of the Empire pleased her enormously. In the minds of most Britons – and indeed, around the world – the mighty Empire was personified by a small woman dressed in black, usually flanked by one or more of her many children.

FAULT LINES

IN 1897, VICTORIA ONLY RELUCTANTLY prepared to celebrate an unprecedented sixty years on the throne. Although mindful of the significance, both symbolic and political, of the event, she loathed having to feature in public spectacle, and had done so since the tragic early loss of her beloved Albert.

The period was also marked, as we have seen, by the Great Agricultural Depression, largely caused by a series of poor harvests and increased international competition thanks to better and faster transport – from about 1873 till 1896. It is important to note that as the nation had undergone industrialisation, there were many differences – across Party and class lines especially – in views of how to approach the problem of class unrest and inherent inequality, although there was, increasingly in the late Victorian period, a shared conviction that the working and struggling classes needed encouragement to improve their lot. There was also a growing awareness of the inherent conflict between better conditions – better pay, notably – and profit maximisation. As other nations such as America, Germany, France and Japan caught up to rival Britain's economic dominance, industrialists and landowners sought to safeguard their investments. As the labour movement gained traction, calls for reform grew.

There was thus an appreciation, among the more informed and intelligent ruling elite, of the problems that simmered below the surface.

Mining strikes were a regular feature of national life, gaining much publicity and, often, considerable sympathy. Agitations for Home Rule in Ireland and rebellions in India and South Africa put paid to any notion that the Empire was impregnable. Pressure to reduce military spending had become a commonplace amid competing budgets and demands for low taxes. Liberal, Conservative and Radical politicians were all too aware of the fault lines below the surface. The rise of the Irish Nationalist Party, led by the charismatic and dangerously clubbable Irish Protestant landowner Charles Stewart Parnell, was a tangible sign that politics as usual was not going to be sustainable in the long term, despite the conventional appetite for a traditional society upheld by a prosperous and stable economy.

No observant politician could ignore imperial fault lines at the time of the Diamond Jubilee. An ill-fated, unauthorised expedition to Benin City, led by the Deputy Commissioner and Consul for the Niger Coast Protectorate, James Phillips, ended in catastrophe and massacre. A punitive expedition was then launched in February 1897, resulting in the summary deposition of the ruler and a trial headed by a British judge sent out for that purpose. The result was a shameful episode in British history: Benin City was captured, and the kingdom was presently absorbed into colonial Nigeria. There were long-term consequences, with the British press baying for blood.

The Royal Niger Company's charter was revoked in December 1899, and the Company sold its holdings to the British Government; the following month all the British Crown-amassed territories and holdings, and the confiscated territories, along with the Niger Coast Protectorate, were amalgamated into the Northern and Southern Protectorates of the Niger River. This land and resources grab set the tone for much of the 'Scramble for Africa' undertaken by leading European nations and, in addition to the obvious ethical questions, meant that the responsibility for ensuring that British trade and protecting the colonies laid a heavy burden on the state.[29]

So despite any underlying worries about imperial reach and the uglier realities of colonial exploitation, the nation, as a whole, defaulted to the dominant emotion,[30] and to the dominant value of, if not quite jingoism, certainly a rallying to the flag and support of the British Empire. Led by commercial interests and aggressive expansionism, the adoption of an Empire had many unforeseen consequences, however, with one of the most salient being that the economic imperative led government policy. Trade, and support for the state in the form of the Empire, became one of the only features of foreign policy and British nationalism that was consistent through the socio-economic groups.

And there was sincere belief in the mission: as Britain extended and consolidated imperial reach, works of engineering were seen as improvements. In the September of this Jubilee year, it was reported that a 'March of Civilisation' was taking place in the Sudan. A full page of illustrations featured in the popular *Illustrated London News* depicting Sudanese workers 'laying cable and testing a handset' and others labouring to create a 'Permanent Way of the Nubian Desert Railway'. Sudanese workers carried and laid tracks, alongside 'a locomotive blowing steam'. Ominously, in a picture that spoke a thousand words demonstrating that lessons had not been learnt, a 'Uniformed Sudanese officer' was shown brandishing a whip.[31]

THE CHARMED CIRCLE

THE PRINCE OF WALES WAS NATURALLY a huge draw for the Jubilee Ball, and provided just the right kind of social cachet as well as an ebullient enthusiasm for the fancy-dress theme. His enthusiastic endorsement and, indeed, championing of the Ball project guaranteed its exclusivity. With the royals on board, Louise,[32] Duchess of Devonshire, could take an ambitious look at the political elite for her guest list. At the time, the ruling class was still overwhelmingly dominated by the landed aristocracy. There had been some changes, as previously discussed, in the economic conditions within the Empire which had shifted in favour of those creating new sources of wealth. As has been observed, the 'charmed circle' was no longer, by 1897, 'confined to families which owned landed estates, although those formed its core'. The privileged elite opened up beyond the 'wider cousinhood of those descended from or connected to landed families, who were frequently to be found in the Church, the army and navy, the diplomatic service, and the law'.[33]

The elite now included a greater number of foreigners, including many Americans. There had always been within the social elite 'a small element of newcomers who were welcomed into the circle, customarily as brides, but occasionally as grooms, by virtue of their wealth and acquired graces'.[34] This number increased, especially under the patronage of the Prince of Wales, who was drawn to the excitement, novelty and beauty that rich newcomers brought to his life and entourage. Also within this group was a set of wildly successful manufacturers and retailers.

The manufacturing industry and the world of finance were steadily replacing land as the most powerful engines of wealth creation. Indeed, manufacturing 'occupied the centre of the stage in the industrial economy which was consolidated during the Victorian period. Machines, factories, and power were the key elements in innovation and productivity growth, and catch the eye of the historian as they did of contemporaries on account of their novelty, modernity and success.'[35]

As the economic activities changed and evolved, not all the ensuing developments were welcome. The contraction of the agricultural industry, for example, resulted in a decline in the relative share of the labour force engaged in agriculture: it declined from 25 to 20 per cent from 1831 to 1851, and further dropped to under 9 per cent by 1901.[36] Redistribution of manpower took place in the service sectors of the economy, commerce, transport, the professions, and central and local government service; some of it was in mining and quarrying, and building and construction, usually classed as non-manufacturing industries. This represented huge changes to the traditional ways of life. It meant people relocating to other (often urban) environments, uprooting from local communities and stability, and generally facing challenges unfamiliar hitherto.

Because of the overall adaptability of the population in absorbing these changes and investing their labour in activity other than agriculture, much

Lord Wolverton as King Richard, Coeur de Lion

of the contraction and agricultural depression since the 1870s was balanced by other, healthier parts of the economy. As industrialisation continued, there were generally rising incomes in certain sectors.[37] That being said, there was still enormous wealth in the landed sector. As the 'traditional and firmly established upper class', large landowners

> remained socially paramount until the First World War, their social leadership slightly diluted but not seriously challenged, and socially dominant until a gradual rather than precipitate decline set in from the 1880s. The old order remained, therefore, the top layer of Victorian society, even while all the time a new order was being shaped by the forces of urbanization and industrialization.[38]

Given that the traditional landed class still held most of the cards by which the political game was played, and because, as has been astutely observed, 'the habits of accepting landed leadership long outlasted the radical alterations in the rules by the Third Reform Act of 1884–5 and the 1888 County Councils Act', this privileged elite had, in order to survive as dominant players, to take care in how it chose to exercise power. It was not acceptable to govern 'in a narrowly self-interested way' but imperative to take 'broad account of the needs and wishes of the middle classes, and from time to time of the working classes'.[39]

And although landed wealth had long been the single most important element of wealth in Britain, within the acreage there were huge variations in quantity and quality of land, in its situation and thus its value. Since one of the most important characteristics of land ownership was its ability to generate income, these variations were hugely significant, especially as until the late nineteenth century – and thus at the time of the Jubilee Ball – 'the great landowners were the wealthiest men in the kingdom'.[40]

Of these massively rich men, the top ten controlled vast amounts of Britain's wealth.

Gross Landed Incomes in £ in 1883: [41]

1. Duke of Westminster, approximately 290–323,000
2. Duke of Buccleuch and Queensberry, 232,000
3. Duke of Bedford, approximately 225–250,000
4. Duke of Devonshire, 181,000
5. Duke of Northumberland, 176,000
6. Earl of Derby, 163,000
7. Marquess of Bute, 153,000
8. Duke of Sutherland, 142,000
9. Duke of Hamilton and Brandon, 141,000
10. Earl Fitzwilliam, 139,000

The Dukes of Londonderry and Portland were not far behind. It is important to bear in mind that these amounts are annual income, and should give us an idea of the vast amounts of money coming into the coffers of these families. When we look at the arrival of 'new money' into the court and into the political, social and cultural establishment, it is, therefore, crucial to remember that even with the vast influxes of cash these newcomers brought, 'the capital value of the holdings of the richest landowners exceeded the total wealth of the richest businessmen down to the First World War or even later'. [42]

We will see, through analysing the Jubilee Ball, that although electoral reforms in the latter part of the nineteenth century had widened enfranchisement and improved electoral practice, what had not really changed was the sense of how the nation was led, and by whom. The House of Lords remained a bastion of the traditional landed aristocracy (though the creation of new peerages began to include successful businessmen, from whom a succession of prime ministers sought support). The House of Commons was still overwhelmingly elitist – with the tiniest minority drawn from the working class, and the bulk of members from the aristocracy, who could afford to work for no pay (MPs were not remunerated until 1912).

Representatives from such professions as the law, traditionally dominated by the public-school elite, completed this privileged group. Further, despite the massive economic changes wrought by the Industrial Revolution, there remained a scarcity of businessmen at the helm of the country. Louise was therefore able to choose her political guests with ease, since they were, with few exceptions, members of her social set.

SPEND, SPEND, SPEND

MUCH LIKE TODAY, BRITAIN'S PROSPERITY in 1897 was based on consumer spending. The economy's success was predicated on a society of growing consumption, where the replication of goods and services enjoyed by the privileged few was duplicated more cheaply to be purchased in ever-increasing quantity by mass markets. Like cheap taxis, home restaurant services, inexpensive throwaway fashion and the ubiquitous ease of instant messaging, the luxury of using private chauffeurs, chefs, designer clothing and frequent telegraphing was now available to all but the poorest in British society.

The origins of this materialist culture can be traced in large part to the Industrial Revolution, of course, but also to the Great Exhibition of 1851. This enormously successful venture, the brainchild of a foreigner, Prince Albert, launched – or indeed, reinforced – a trend in Victorian Britain to encourage consumption. The laudable objective of showcasing the nation's most admirable products was achieved, but so, too, was the exhortation to the thousands of visitors, and to the many more thousands who read about the wares and admired the pictures, to buy, and to buy more.

The way to prosperity, at home and abroad, was to produce British goods as efficiently as possible, and to sell them in high volume. Supply was well under way, but to increase demand, consumers had to desire the products so much that they would work hard to have them. The inherent mind-set of the ruling elite was that all classes would ultimately benefit by the successful production, promotion, purchase and export of British goods. As the lower classes worked hard to 'better' themselves (i.e. consume more), they needed motivation to do so. A better life must equate to a life of material prosperity – which a stable, strong and secure economy could provide.

Security and stability had been watchwords among Britain's ruling classes, especially after observing with horror the revolutionary throes of continental Europe throughout the nineteenth century, and it formed a guiding principle of British public and private life. The rise of the Radical movement had led to social reforms and had widened suffrage, but even radical politicians such as the Birmingham manufacturer Joseph Chamberlain were staunch imperialists.

Stability was good for the economy, the royals were good for stability, and people of all classes celebrated the Diamond Jubilee nationwide with joy and excitement. Parades, street parties, bunting, floral displays in the major towns and cities, electrical illuminations (London was particularly magnificent), were accompanied by an avalanche of publicity, and royal and aristocratic visitors. Souvenirs, commemorative medals and jewellery were produced to celebrate the British Empire and its Queen. As with the Golden Jubilee in 1887, this was a marvellous opportunity to promote Britain and to demonstrate strength to the colonies and to neighbours. The festivities drew thousands of wealthy visitors, and British manufacturers and retailers rushed to crowd the market with jubilee-themed tonics, soaps, teas, fabrics and commemorative medals and jewellery.

The star of the show, Victoria, though, had had to be coaxed and coerced into getting in any way involved in the Golden Jubilee ten years previously – and was particularly aghast at the thought of the relations coming to celebrate. For the Diamond Jubilee, the Queen firmly put her small foot down and recommended a ban on all reigning monarchs – in this way she would not have to house and feed them all, and would avoid contact with her eldest grandchild, Kaiser Wilhelm II, whom she disliked. Although Cabinet members were dismayed at this intransigence, the resulting vacuum provided an opportunity to shift the focus of events on to the colonies rather than the continental rulers.

On 26 June, the great naval review was held. This was intended to impress the watching world with the Empire's dominance. Although naval reviews had been a feature of major landmarks and celebrations, it was felt that 'no review in Great Britain or abroad has ever been – looked at, at least, from the spectacular point of view – so magnificent as that of Saturday last'. Even though a similar number of ships might have been present, 'no fleet heretofore assembled in any waters has been so powerful or composed in so large a proportion of the newest and latest types of vessels'. It was also believed that 'no previous fleet was possessed of the peculiar significance which attaches to this fleet of her Majesty's Diamond Jubilee year'.

First, the powerful display represented, according to the press,

> the results of the nation's complete awakening to the real value of sea power and of all that it entails to an Empire such as ours; and secondly, an evidence to the assembled Empire that the Mother-country has recognised her duties and responsibilities, and has not been unfaithful to her trust. It was also in a special sense a demonstration to the world that Great Britain duly values all that her Navy has given her, and intends to retain it, no matter the cost. [43i]

Further, the audience – colonial and foreign,

> were impressed and, indeed, startled by what we were able to show them; and it may be suspected that even we ourselves were somewhat surprised to see the magnitude and perfection of the great machine which we have of late created . . .
>
> Thanks to the carefulness and ability of Staff-Commander Hawkins-Smith, the Master of the Fleet, berths were found at Spithead for the 160 or 170 vessels composing the Fleet [without withdrawing a single ship from a foreign station], and the British ships were arranged in four long and two short lines, stretching from near Horse Fort on the east to the neighbourhood of the Bramble on the west. The total length of these lines was twenty-eight or thirty miles.[43ii]

Mrs Arthur Sassoon as La Dogeressa

The link with the Queen and royal family was strongly made as the Royal Yacht, with the Prince of Wales and other royals aboard, toured the fleet. Each vessel struck up – with a band if they had one – 'God Save the Queen' as the yacht, flying the Royal Standard, passed by, and sailors saluted. That evening, a glorious festival of illumination of all the vessels – including foreign ones – took place, thrilling the crowds, with fireworks and rocket flares lighting up the heavens. As one journalist commented:

> It has been a day never to be forgotten. All who were present must have come away with new ideas as to what this great Empire means both to us and to others; and it can hardly be that a demonstration so splendid can fail in furthering to a very great degree two principal objects for which it was arranged. One of these was to prove that Britain still rules the waves and, moreover, intends to go on ruling them; the other was to show to our fellow-subjects in the outlying parts of the Empire that they have with us a common possession to be proud of and to depend upon in the hour of need.[44]

Colonial Secretary Chamberlain was keen to capitalise on such a demonstration of strength and invited all eleven prime ministers of the Empire's self-governing colonies to attend a gathering that was the predecessor of the twentieth-century Commonwealth conference. Indian princes as well as representative military escorts from Canada, New Zealand and the several Australian colonies were joined by Indian army troops and detachments from Malta, Trinidad, Natal and other dependencies to form part of the magnificent parade due to take place through the capital on Jubilee Day. And Chamberlain was quick to seize the advantageous platform provided by the Jubilee to promote his views on a common trading agreement within the Empire. It was reported that the Colonial Secretary 'looks forward to four or five weeks of discussion with the Colonial Premiers before they leave London, and he will find them practically unanimous in their demand for the removal of the hindrances to closer inter-Imperial relations which the Belgian and German treaties now create'.[45]

Despite the Queen's reluctance to go to any effort herself, the proposed celebrations attracted enormous interest abroad. Continental princes, innumerable foreign ambassadors and members of Victoria's large extended family clamoured for invitations to the most prestigious events. Rich Americans planned their trips with military precision, booking the luxury hotels and snapping up the best viewing spots for sale on the specially constructed stands. Homes and clubs sold access to balconies and windows to eager spectators as food and drink vendors prepared their wares. Hotel owners, restaurateurs and shopkeepers rejoiced.

For the government, it was out of the question not to profit from the message of strength, security and stability that the Jubilee would represent. If well directed, the nation could display on a world stage her pre-eminence and her seemingly unassailable position as the number one global superpower. With her superlative navy and resplendent army, Britain was the world's greatest trader and dominated vast quantities of territory. However much staid traditionalists such as Prime Minister Gladstone and Lord Salisbury might privately deprecate the vulgarity and jingoism provoked by the celebration of the Jubilee, there was too much at stake to do anything other than play the imperialist game.

It was increasingly a challenge, however. Britain's determination to remain the sole global superpower was becoming increasingly ambitious, as other industrialised nations developed rapidly and challenged her markets. The appeal of cheaper imports was self-evident, but it provided all kinds of additional challenges for Britain's manufacturers – and for her self-governing colonies, who persuasively argued for preferential tariffs in return for their loyalty, and for their contribution to Britain's hugely expensive navy. There was, naturally, a marked reluctance across the political spectrum to impose higher taxes on the nation to pay for the defence of the Empire and her markets. Even senior Liberals began to look more and more to the wealthy landed aristocrats to take up a larger share of the financial burden.

The real problem, though, was the threat of war and the cost of protecting imperial routes as well as territories. Conflict was always expensive. Already by 1897 there were skirmishes in South Africa (where the Queen wanted to send more troops), India and Afghanistan. Rumblings from far-flung corners of the Empire competed with land agitation and violence in nearby Ireland for political and military attention. As Victoria fretted, ministers disagreed privately on whether the cost of the Empire was sustainable and how to improve living conditions for the very poorest at home and in British territories.

The threat of social unrest, of higher taxes, of rebellion in the colonies and dependencies, along with increased aggression and competition from Germany and other powers, combined to dampen some of the spirits of the ruling class. With privilege came responsibility, of which public service was an expectation. If the ruling class were to lead by example, they would make their consumption public, recorded in the media, and it would be conspicuous: if they were not exclusively practising a 'buy British' campaign, they could and would 'bat for Britain'. As Daisy Warwick observed, in this the social elite were aided and abetted by the press, where their 'every extravagance was held up to the public as a proper expenditure of money – it was good for trade!'

In her view, this 'strengthened the position of our circle, because it made us a privileged class'. Indeed, their patronage 'was sought by tradesmen, eager to satisfy our every caprice for the honour of serving us, while waiting indefinitely for our money'. Astonishingly, during the period, bills were presented yearly – or in some cases triennially. Since, as she pointed out, the middle classes 'were always led by the aristocracy', this meant that an endorsement by an aristocrat of those outside the magic circle was treated with the same deference, and their 'money was strangely like that of their more blue-blooded brethren'. The amounts of money spent – especially on clothing – were colossal, and Daisy believed that there could be 'little doubt' that this reliance on revenue by this high-spending group 'encouraged an unyielding conservatism among the shopkeepers, and gave the trading community a horror of those whom the aristocracy abhorred – the wicked Radicals'.[46]

PATRIOTIC FERVOUR

With its magnificence and splendour, the Diamond Jubilee marked what is now seen as a high mark of patriotic fervour. A scant five years later, Chamberlain addressed the 1902 Colonial Conference referring to 'the weary Titan' which staggered 'under the too vast orb of its fate'.[47] And indeed, there was, in some quarters, already a murmuring anxiety over the expense and effort of governing one-quarter of the globe and over 400 million people. What made the imperial engine run was, of course, the people driving it. Every subject had an implicit part to play in maintaining the success of the British Business Enterprise, and it is fascinating to see how the need of the elite to show off was channelled to so neatly correspond to the need of the population to witness them doing so. A devil's bargain, no doubt, especially for someone like Hartington, a quiet man who had inherited less than people generally believed and who longed for privacy, but a bargain of necessity.

In a hauntingly familiar tale, as mass media invaded every part of their private lives, some aristocrats increasingly used the press – and were used by them in turn. Scandals were particularly delectable fare and the public lapped up every detail fulsomely reported in magazines and newspapers. Editors who had previously treated their social superiors with deference began recruiting eager journalists with an eye for thrilling copy. At the same time, many of these privileged celebrities were running low on funds after land rents declined in the last quarter of the century, and there were few options available to them to solve the problem. What had previously been a notoriously closed and private aristocratic world began to open somewhat – and to show cracks.

The development of media that provided salacious details of the lives of the upper classes was one that had not at first unduly alarmed the elite. Professional beauties, as they were known, such as Jennie Churchill and the Prince of Wales's lover Lillie Langtry were happy to have their photographs published, and retailers delighted in promoting their wares by association. The rise of mid-market publications was seen by traditionalists

such as Lord Salisbury as a deplorable trend. He famously referred to the
Daily Mail as 'a paper written by office boys for office boys'. That was all
very well, but the paper, founded in 1896 by Alfred Harmsworth (later
1st Viscount Northcliffe), was immensely popular, reaching a circulation
of one million by 1902. The most wealthy patricians deplored the advent
of cheap journalism, which they considered the emblem of 'the corrupting
forces which were at work in British society'.[48]

But other high-status families could not afford to be so sniffy. Many
simply needed money and were introduced to this new world of shifting
values. Men of varying talents such as Jack Churchill were ushered by Bertie's
pal, the financier Sir Ernest Cassel, into City firms, with highly variable
rates of success. Others such as Lord Lonsdale (the 'Yellow Earl'), who
sought to make his fortune by investing in cattle in the American West, lost
everything – before inheriting a family fortune. The Dukes of Marlborough
and Manchester, and George Curzon, married wealthy American heiresses.
For the women, the options were even more limited, and a great number
of them wrote books. These were usually autobiographies, written with
greater or lesser discretion. Scandals revealed sold more, but lost one friends.

Royal watching and gaping at the aristocracy had become a spectator
sport by the time of the Diamond Jubilee, and in this the voracious public
appetite was encouraged by rapid developments in photographic technology
and availability of prints for sale. At the time of the Devonshire Ball,
several professional photographers moved to London. James Stack Lauder
– who had, somewhat mendaciously, traded as 'Lafayette, late of Paris' in
Dublin since 1885 – had premises in New Bond Street, one of the capital's
most luxurious shopping streets. Louise, in a daring move, commissioned
Lafayette to photograph those attending the Ball, and had a special tent set
up in the garden to take individual pictures of all the guests in their finery.
This innovation proved immensely popular, and such was the demand that
many of the guests visited the studio over the following six months, to be
immortalised in their costumes.

It was especially exciting to be photographed on the occasion of the
Diamond Jubilee, as it was also the first royal state celebration to be

Mr Arthur Sassoon as Chief of the Janissaries

captured in moving film. Although still in its very early development, the film-making industry was growing. Many film-makers from around the world gathered in London to film the great event. There were around forty cameras lining the procession route and 'an astonished audience in Bradford' were the first to view Britain's first same-day newsreel.[49]

Those of Bertie's circle willing to play the game sold more than copy. An ostentatious aristocratic lifestyle was put on display, and it led to aspirational desires as much as that of celebrities, sportspeople and movie stars does today. Glimpses of fabulous furnishings, exquisite jewellery, stunning apparel and vistas of the rich leading perfect lives resulted in readers' ambitions to emulate these mythical creatures. And, as a lipstick sells a dream, cheaper copies of goods became ever more desirable. This was not the only imitation at play: instead of collecting and showing off selfies, readers cut out pictures of the stars from magazines and newspapers and carefully preserved them. Avid admirers could even purchase photographs of aristocratic 'Society Beauties'. After pictures were published showing Bertie's fashionable wife's 'wall of friends', composed of a shelf entirely covered in photographs in silver frames of her intimates, it became a fashion much imitated by the middle classes. Much to the horror of the Queen and the aristocratic contingent faithful to the traditional virtues of discretion, it insidiously became an expectation for the privileged to play their part in providing these audiences of potential consumers with aspirational examples of what money, luck and hard work could provide.

As the aristocracy continued to legitimise privilege and power in the old-fashioned sense, the needs and expectations of wider society were changing and those trapped by birth on the lower socio-economic rungs wanted their betters to be visibly attractive. Where British aristocrats such as the 8th Duke of Devonshire had for years never given much thought to how he was perceived by others, he had – as others like him – been assigned a role above and beyond the traditional duty of public service. It was no longer enough, by the 1890s, for leading aristocrats to serve the nation: they must also be seen by the public at large to be doing so. These demands increased as the population shifted from rural to urban environments (by 1901 fully

80 per cent of the population was urbanised), and it became even more important for traditional societal structures to be articulated and reinforced. This compact was indefatigably promoted by the press: magazines and newspapers relied on larger-than-life characters such as Harty Tarty and the Double Duchess, as the Duke and Duchess of Devonshire were known, to sell the British way of life.

The story of the legendary Devonshire ball explores the extraordinary characters who attended, and the complex and at times downright bewildering array of personal relationships that united to 'battle for Britain'. These men and women were friends and enemies; they flirted with, courted and married one another, conducted clandestine love affairs and barely disguised feuds, and governed the Empire from famous mansions and country houses as much as from Westminster.

III

POWER AND PURPOSE

THE MEDIA WERE AGOG AS NEWS OF THE SPLENDID BALL filtered through. Titbits from the excited guests were shared with journalists, who breathlessly wrote of the planned celebrations:

> For weeks … much popular interest has been evoked as the details have been disclosed of preparations for an ambitious achievement being brought to the utmost perfection, to culminate in a galaxy of splendour destined to be the crowning effect of the multifarious efforts to render resplendent the glories of her Majesty's Diamond Jubilee – an historical pageant designed by the noble hosts to commemorate this unique event of her Majesty's reign.[50]

Celebrations and entertainments such as masquerades and fancy-dress balls had been for centuries a prominent feature of English life. Festivities including a 'masque' had been a popular entertainment at the royal court since before the Tudor reign. A long tradition of using disguise and spectacle had evolved amongst the upper classes; as early as 1606 such a celebration took place for the 'very grand wedding' in the Chapel Royal in Whitehall. The bride, 'an extraordinarily beautiful girl of fifteen', was Lady Frances Howard, the younger daughter of Thomas Howard, Earl of Suffolk. He was 'one of the highest-ranking officials at the court of King James I of England', and the groom was the noble Robert Devereux, 3rd Earl of Essex.

To mark such an exalted union, an elaborate masque, featuring music, poetry and dance, was staged in the Banqueting House, Whitehall. Whereas in Queen Elizabeth's day such entertainments had been modest presentations, after the accession of James I the fashion grew for much more extravagant entertainments, for which large budgets for costumes and sets were dedicated.[51] There was, on a less grandiose level, also a long history of village fetes and high-spirited 'holydays' where workers enjoyed an all too rare day of unfettered joy.[52]

Middle-class families were drawn to public spectacle, paying for tickets to watch entertainments and, indeed, buying costumes and dressing up themselves. The latter, however, given its cost, was more a feature of upper-class life, and, especially of country house living, where charades and other party games were very popular. In other entertainments, opera- and theatre-goers – in the cities a cross-section of the inhabitants – enjoyed evenings where assumed identities on stage provided escapist pleasure.

Masquerades proper were introduced to London by the Swiss count Johann Jacob Heidegger, an impresario who first came across them in Italy and originally staged them in London theatres. Although he was appointed as Master of the Revels to George II, thus acquiring a royal endorsement, there was nevertheless a great deal of consternation at the subversive nature of the masquerade, and a backlash against such entertainments throughout the eighteenth century.[53] The attractive and glamorous masquerades were perceived by moral authorities such as Edward Gibson, the Bishop of London, as deviant and dangerous.

But the entertainments remained hugely popular. In London, Vauxhall Gardens opened to the paying public in 1729 (and, later, Ranelagh Gardens, in 1741); they became sought-after destinations for those who could afford it. Masquerades became part of spectacles staged to celebrate significant public events, such as the end of a war or a royal birthday. In 1749, Vauxhall hosted a masquerade to mark the Treaty of Aix-la-Chapelle, which concluded the War of the Austrian Succession.

Although the masquerade's popularity declined, 'fancy-dress balls' remained a form of fashionable entertainment throughout the nineteenth century. Embraced with enthusiasm by the wealthy with plenty of disposable income, these entertainments were quite respectable, and bore little resemblance to the racy masquerades of yore. Another outlet for disguise was the cult of private theatricals, hosted in country homes. It is interesting to note the accounts in well-known novels of the period, such as *Mansfield Park*,

Villette, *Vanity Fair*, *Pride and Prejudice* and *Jane Eyre*, which feature charades and dressing up.[54]

The appeal of fancy-dress balls spread to the aspiring middle classes, who, as their purchasing power increased, drove mass production of fancy-dress goods. The market was further served by the arrival and development of department stores, where customers could meet all their needs under one roof. Manuals to educate consumers on fashion tips and advice proliferated. Ladies' magazines provided extensive cover of the latest fashions, and experts such as Ardern Holt, under the auspices of his employer, the department emporium Debenham & Freebody, wrote book-length advice pieces. 'Fancy Dresses Described' was so popular that it went through six editions from 1879 to 1896, handsomely illustrated and extremely attractive. Such was the popularity of the books that in 1882 Holt produced a companion book for men's fancy dress as well.

This growing revival of public dancing – albeit in very private and exclusive venues – was aided by a young Queen Victoria after her coronation in 1837, when the waltz was at its most popular. Victoria had received dancing lessons as a child, and her coronation provided the opportunity for three State balls to take place. Her marriage to Albert in 1840 was marked by a further series of parties, including balls. The Queen and Prince gave a number of fancy-dress balls, including one at which she wore a bodice studded with diamonds. Victoria's love of dancing – and her husband Albert was a very accomplished dancer himself – ushered in an era of enthusiasm for dance.

New dances, such as the volta from Poland, were introduced, although it was said that the waltz remained the Queen's favourite. The upper classes reprised the earlier popularity of dancing, and dances played an important role in the courtship process, the success of which was integral to the continuation of a strong patriarchal society, predicated on primogeniture. In order to preserve the moral rectitude demanded by the monarch, fancy-dress, or costume, balls replaced the more risqué masquerade. Thus the choice for a fancy-dress ball to mark the first diamond jubilee of a British monarch was a fitting one, integrating centuries of historical narrative with nineteenth-century tastes for dressing up and for theatricals.

The Earl of Rosebery as a gentleman of the eighteenth century

Fancy-dress balls gained in popularity, and newspapers regularly contained advertisements for ticketed fancy-dress balls throughout the nation. Those in costume usually had discounted tickets. Fancy-dress balls for children often had prizes for the best outfit. The skating rink, 'Niagara', at St James's Park was famous for its aristocratic patronage (Prince Hans Heinrich and Princess Daisy of Pless skated there daily when in London) and its fancy-dress parties. Vivid accounts of the beautiful costumes, live orchestra and brilliant lighting featured in breathless press accounts. Fancy-dress parties and glamorous balls were a feature of aristocratic life – the season was so filled with events that many followed in the steps of the Prince of Wales to take a cure in Homberg or the South of France – favoured by the Duchess of Devonshire.

EXTRAVAGANCE AND GLAMOUR

It rapidly became clear, as news of the Jubilee Ball spread, that it was to be an extravaganza like no other, and that only the most favoured would be among the guests. Invitations thus carried enormous social, cultural and political currency. Tales abounded of would-be guests languishing in hope of the arrival of an invitation. 'The Duchess is worried daily for invitations,' reported one newspaper: 'Six hundred were issued, and that is somewhat overtaxing the resources of the mansion should the weather render the illuminated gardens impracticable. Now numbers of people are begging and praying to be asked, actually urging that they have had dresses made in the full expectation that they would be.'[55] 'A well-connected American' told the tale of one 'foreign lady who moved heaven and earth to get herself invited, finally appealing to her country's ambassador.' Apparently 'His Excellency' made an appeal to the hostess, who was, however, 'like flint: her list was closed'. After a pause, however, came a dagger blow from the Duchess: 'If she likes to come without a card she may come.'[56]

This ball was to play an important part of the total display being presented by Britain to the world. The Jubilee celebrations were important for the colonial representatives, for the foreign royalties and dignitaries, and for the nation at large, to witness a successful and self-confident, prosperous Empire, a country open for business and keen to create and perpetuate a financial regime in which one could have confidence. Investment – both financial and political – could be safely made in Britain's economy, in a united, stable nation that favoured trade and enabled its facilitation. This was one of the most important objectives of the Ball: Britain lived on its maritime success and its trade. The government debates of the era centred on tariffs or free trade – but there was no question about the importance of import and export.

The greater spending power of larger sections of the population, notably of the burgeoning middle class, provided yet more impetus to the luxury producers and consumers to attain ever greater achievements. Tailors, dressmakers, milliners, theatrical costumiers, cobblers, jewellers, haberdashers, manufacturers of accessories such as gloves, hosiery, parasols, scarves and fans, profited by the explosion of demand for fine goods. The aristocracy and economic and social elite led the way, their garments copied at lesser cost for the broader community.

As was the case for most things artistic, France was considered the gold standard for fashion. Despite efforts made earlier in the century to 'buy British', the most fashionable – and well-off – looked to Paris for their *haute couture*. Such slavish worship of all things French had irritated Queen Adelaide to such an extent that, immediately after William IV had ascended the throne in 1830, she had announced her intention of banning the wearing of French confections at court.[57] This 'Buy British' campaign had been launched to combat the post-war slump of 1826–30 in the home textile and fashion industries. The removal of the ban on foreign-made gloves in 1825, for example, had 'flooded the market with cheap German imports and chic French "kids"'.[58]

And the decline of Britain's lace industry was vividly exemplified when a wedding gown commissioned for Queen Victoria's marriage in 1840 was sourced with difficulty, as there was such a scarcity of lace-makers to produce the gown of Honiton sprigs.[59] The traditional wares of tailoring and dressmaking trades, such as fine haberdashery, had commanded more allure if imported from France. Advertisements proliferated offering, for example, the newest and most fashionable artificial flowers, fancy feathers, silk and gold buttons and many other novelties from the French capital. Exhortations to buy British mostly fell on deaf ears when it came to cutting a dash in the world of fashion. A long and rich tradition of fashion finery in France consistently proved serious competition to indigenous producers.

As today, when celebrity ensembles are quickly replicated and worn by thousands, the aspirational members of the nation bought cheaper copies of what the elite were wearing. The novelist Ouida acidly commented on the arrival of excursion trains to Derbyshire beauty spots, filled with 'townies', including 'women with dress that "aped the fashion"'.[60] But the increasing appetite for, and ability to finance, consumption was the capitalist mantra on which Britain's economic success was predicated. The Devonshire House Ball was but one major example of the ruling class providing an example of showing what money could buy. Guests spent a fortune on garments, gems and accessories – and a pageant packed with visual cues to power, pleasure and predominance served the second purpose of 'helping' Britain's economy.

The well-publicised Ball reinforced the nation's passion for shopping. The retail sector was growing significantly and the offer was opening up to the middle classes: in the 1860s and 1870s major department stores, for example, became increasingly important. Businesses such as Whiteley's in Bayswater, Harrods in Knightsbridge, Barkers in Kensington, along with Broadbent's in Southport and Lewis's in Liverpool, transformed from grocery and drapers' shops into huge emporiums.

Pictures that proliferated through the newspapers and magazines of a lovely dress or hat or shoes or a fan or some other accessory piqued the desire of less wealthy people to become actors in a similar play. From the capital to the smaller cities, towns and countryside, the appetite for the latest fashions – especially those from Paris, the acknowledged leader of all things artistic and fashionable – grew exponentially.

Paste replicas of jewellery proliferated. The market for fashion accessories was enormous, and shopkeepers laid-in large quantities of jewels in anticipation of Jubilee spending. For the Ball, many of the wealthy society leaders had their jewels reset to give historical authenticity to their costumes. It was in fact a point of pride to have sufficient gems to create enough of an effect – a sentiment later, famously, echoed by Julian Fellowes. In his account of attending the Academy Awards in 2002, he asserted that his wife Emma was, he was 'fairly sure, the only woman there who owned her own frock and jewels'.[61]

Those who did not have a safe full of fabulous jewellery turned to the high-end retailers of London. It was reported that for the Devonshire House Ball 'Metropolitan jewellers charged as much as £50 for the loan of one ornament for the night, while several people borrowed from £10,000 to £20,000 worth of precious stones for the occasion'.[62] Dressmakers, designers, artists, accessory-makers and others were pressed into service and business boomed. In addition to the more expected providers, theatres played their part. The Alhambra Theatre was well represented. Its official costumier, Alias, 'provided the dresses of the Prince of Wales, the Duke of Connaught, and a hundred others'.[63]

The ballet master Signor Carlo Coppi had been prevailed upon to arrange and supervise the procession of the different courts, and the intricate quadrilles performed by some of the guests, to great effect. And for what was one of the most innovative and dramatic costumes of the night, the celebrated singer (and well-known socialite) Fanny Ronalds wore a costume invented by the chief electrician of the Alhambra. Mr Webber created a dress representing, fittingly, the Muse of Music, for which he remained the entire evening in attendance to charge up the illuminating lights that flickered throughout the Ball. Although the fancy dress was an indubitable success, the American singer – foreshadowing today's electric vehicles – had to disappear regularly behind the scenes to get the lights re-charged.[64]

IV
THE EXTRAVAGANZA

As *THE TIMES* BREATHLESSLY reported, the party reached a peak at around 11 o'clock:

> the **National Anthem announced the arrival of the Royal party**, who were dressed, like the rest of the company, in character, and some of whose costumes we describe elsewhere. They took their seats on the dais, and immediately the **'processions' began**, each Court advancing in order, bowing, and passing on. This over, the **quadrilles began** – very stately and sumptuous, the Italian quadrille perhaps bearing the palm. Nothing more harmonious could well be imagined than these **slow dances, walked through by magnificently dressed men and by women whose beauty and jewelled costumes** set off one another with **all the charm of something strange, exceptional, and unique. Waltzes followed,** and a good many of the heroes and heroines were young enough and energetic enough to dance, in spite of unfamiliar cloaks and hats and dresses of strange forms. Then came **lounging in the garden**, which was a **fairyland of lights; supper in the tent**; and the morning hours were well advanced before the **700 guests** had dispersed homewards, to awake to-day upon a world that must indeed seem commonplace in comparison with the jewelled page of romance upon which, for a moment, they gazed last night.[65]

The Jubilee Ball was held in Devonshire House, which had been built in 1735, and stood on one of London's most fashionable sites, on Piccadilly, with a view across Green Park to Buckingham Palace. Devonshire House

Mrs Asquith as an Oriental snake charmer

was built on an enormous scale to an outwardly simple, clean design, facing the rolling lawns of the park. The site was huge, with a frontage to Piccadilly of some 75 yards and a depth of 220 yards. It had been constructed in 1737 on the site of Berkeley House, bought in 1697 by the 1st Duke of Devonshire. The mansion – soon known as Devonshire House – was rebuilt in 1737 after a fire. The famed political hostess and beauty Georgiana, Duchess of Devonshire, had held court here with Charles Fox, Thomas Henry Burke and Richard Brinsley Sheridan in attendance. Devonshire House famously vied with Holland House for over a century as the *de facto* headquarters of the Whig (later, Liberal) Party.

Property was already very costly in London in the nineteenth century, and it grew more and more expensive the closer one came to the centre. The West End was prohibitively dear, and Devonshire House was like a palace on Piccadilly. There were some other splendid mansions in central London that were as large, but none so famous as Devonshire House. And not one could boast of such enormous grounds, which included a forecourt – spacious enough to allow carriages to drive in, deposit guests and exit without doubling back – and gardens that extended to Lansdowne House.

The magnificent, landscaped garden, which stretched up to what is currently Berkeley Square, was one of the property's most famous characteristics, and its rather dull exterior belied the sumptuous and imposing interiors and superb collection of fine furnishings and grand pictures within. The paintings themselves were worthy of a museum collection: superb portraits by Reynolds, Hals, Van Dyck, as well as stunning landscapes by Titian, Poussin, Lancret and Watteau. An *Adoration of the Magi* by Veronese, the *Holy Family with St Elizabeth* by Rubens and *The Story of Samson and Delilah* by Tintoretto were other extraordinary works shown to best advantage in the large, vaulted interiors.[66]

The 8th Duke of Devonshire, or Hartington as he was best known (or 'Harty-Tarty'), had inherited the dukedom in 1891, and had, as we shall see, married his long-time mistress Louise, previously Duchess of Manchester, in 1892. Although he was a notoriously quiet man, who had little taste for society, he loved his wife and provided her with great leeway and an unlimited budget for entertaining as long as he was not expected to go to any trouble himself.

BECAUSE I'M 'WORTH' IT

WORTH WAS THE CLOTHES DESIGNER MOST SOUGHT AFTER by the fashionable set who could afford his sky-high prices. A single gown would fetch between £8,000 and £24,000 in today's money. Such was the reputation of the couturier that the Worth gown was referenced in a book written by the wage reformer Mary Dodge, who stated categorically in her 1872 publication that style could never be considered a necessity. Further, that no woman was under an 'obligation to wear a Worth gown, nor is there real bitterness to the pain of going through life without it'.[67]

Charles Frederick Worth was English by birth, and founded the House of Worth in Paris in 1858. He is considered by many to be the founder of *haute couture*, and ran his fashion house as a very successful business. The House of Worth introduced much innovation as well as superlative design. Clients flocked to his salon, where – in a revolutionary move – Worth had live models demonstrate his creations. A dedicated self-publicist, his fame reached not only the very wealthy clients who patronised his establishment, but the large numbers of women who read about him and his clothing in fashion magazines, where he featured regularly. After his death in 1895, the House was taken over by his son Jean-Philippe, who had worked with the company since 1875.

It was a sign of status and success to become a frequent Worth client, and the designer played up to the image of a gifted artist. Sporting 'velvet caps and capes' raised his 'social profile from mere craftsman to creative genius, a "King of Dress" as one writer dubbed Worth.'[68] There was in the second half of the nineteenth century a consolidation of the international couture market, centred in Paris, undisputedly the art capital of the world. In addition to the French elite, rich buyers from America, Britain and Russia made the pilgrimage to France, where other fashion houses such as Paquin, Doucet, Pingat, Callot and Poiret were based.[69]

Only the wealthiest could patronise these fashion houses. Daisy Warwick recalled that she had twice consulted the House of Worth to commission a costume for fancy-dress balls. Acknowledging that a Worth frock was 'of course, very costly', she wrote that she had 'never had one for which the bill was less than a hundred guineas [about £15,000 today], and often his gowns were half as much again'. Still, the quality of the fabrics, trimmings, lace, furs and other accessories went some way to justifying the expense: 'I always set two facts, that they were the creations of a man of genius, and that the materials would never wear out.'[70]

There was ample room for extravagance, but also for creativity and romance. Many clandestine couples plotted to dress in similar themes, and the constraints of Victorian dress could be ignored by revealing what was usually hidden. Arms and legs were bared, hair flowed loose – and the men who had the inclination and the physique chose to wear skin-tight breeches, or doublets with tights, displaying a shapely leg to best advantage. Playfulness, humour and sex appeal were given free rein. At a time when women still had to observe the strictest codes of modesty in dress and behaviour, the fancy-dress ball provided a socially acceptable occasion to play with the boundaries. Somehow the view of an ankle, loose hair, a deep cleavage was not a social solecism but an enthusiastic gesture of participation.

One of the most amusing activities at the ball was strolling around and gazing at the costumes, many of which were manifestly unbecoming to the wearer. It was difficult for many of the guests to dance because their costumes were heavy, stiff or elaborately fixed in place. Lady Westmorland (*see page 81*) had a magnificent eagle affixed to her shoulder to great effect, but it meant that she was unable to move much.

This marked out the Devonshire House Ball as being different; dancing was habitually one of the greatest attractions of a ball, as it provided a welcome opportunity for men and women to interact in a physical way while enjoying beautiful music. It is believed that the waltz – the most famous and first of the most popular ballroom dances – was introduced to England around 1790.[71] At the time, it was regarded more as a country dance, and this form used the intertwining of the arms stance, rather than the embrace, which followed later. The waltz is documented as having been first performed around 1812 at the famous Almack's Assembly in London.[72] On the night of 2 July, Piccadilly was lined with throngs of spectators, agog to catch a glimpse of the spectacle. Seemingly, no one was immune to the powerful sway of the event, and it was reported that 'Even well-known and very smart people were so curious, and so carried away by the general excitement, that they collected in the courtyard of Devonshire House all among the footmen and other servants assembled…'.[73] The press had for weeks been full of excited articles and gossipy snippets about the fortunate guests – and mock pity for those disappointed individuals who were putting on brave faces or dashing abroad on urgent business. No detail was too small, as magazines and newspapers described the efforts being put into securing the most original and magnificent attire. The event would provide free spectacle, and eager crowds made their way early to Piccadilly to secure the choice viewing spots. Later in the evening, those fortunate to be at the Devonshire House gates craned their necks and climbed on to shoulders to watch the glitterati emerge from their dimly lit carriages. Spectators peeked through the high railings to observe the arrivals to the front entrance, where the Devonshire servants, all of whom were kitted out in period costume with powdered wigs, were in attendance.

One of the important – arguably in many instances the most important – function of those at the apex of the social pyramid, headed by the monarchy, was to inhabit the virtues of the nation. Such virtues, in 1897, were those of power, and pleasure: the upper class at play demonstrated leisure – a luxury – as well as economic might, manifested by incredibly expensive clothing and gems. What we might see as wasteful display of extravagance played the part of showcasing a dominant nation. There was, indeed, a remarkable lack of sniping at the event, despite the fiasco of the Bradley-Martin costume ball held in New York in February of that year. Such was the public opprobrium launched with fury at the Bradley-Martin family that they had fled the United States to escape the virulent personal attacks on what was seen as wanton extravagance. But in Britain, where the Queen, the Empire and the Jubilee were clearly linked to the Ball, there was, rather, admiration and some awe.

In addition to the imaginative costumes, there were the splendid displays of jewellery. Unlike formal state occasions, a fancy-dress ball gave the aristocratic rich a chance to throw good taste and decorum to the winds, and to drape themselves in brilliant and precious gems. Lady Londonderry had many of her family heirlooms re-set. Brilliant diamonds, rubies, emeralds, sapphires, pearls, garnets, tourmalines and others sparkled in the lights, reflecting sparks and creating a magical enchanted fairyland. The 'huge' crystal chandeliers in the great rooms had been carefully dismantled and each crystal re-polished before 'being fitted with new candles',[74] adding to the scintillating, wonderland quality of the night.

The 8th Duke of Devonshire and the Duchess entertained regularly – notably giving a dance held each year on the night after the Derby – and this ball was the most ambitious of their undertakings. It was a tremendous coup for Louise von Alten of Hanover. As we will later explore, it had been quite an impressive life journey for a nineteen-year-old who in 1851 had paraded past Victoria's uncle, the Duke of Cumberland (who had, as per tradition, ascended the Hanoverian throne as King Ernest Augustus on Victoria's accession). Of a noble old Hanoverian family, Louise – tall, blonde and very beautiful, with a perfect profile – featured as one of a series of posed *tableaux vivants*, sitting alone in a huge shell of mother-of-pearl, holding a bouquet of roses. Forty years later, she was one of Britain's foremost political hostesses, aided by a long friendship with the Prince of Wales.

The Duke and Duchess of Devonshire were visible symbols of the very wealthy. His complaints at tax impositions by the Chancellor in 1894 were, unsurprisingly, ill-received. 'The Duke of Devonshire, one of the wealthiest landgrabbers in the world, is suffering from a fit of melancholia because Sir William Harcourt's Budget provides that landlords shall in future pay taxes like other people…. Was ever such a thing heard of? How on earth is the fabulously rich Duke of Devonshire to find money for his race-course orgies, and his country house parties, and the other resources of idling luxury if he pays his taxes?'[75] Giving this incredibly expensive party would do little to curb such ill will.

HH Prince Victor Duleep Singh as Akbar the Great

CAPTURED BY INNOVATION

IN AN ATTEMPT TO HARNESS THE VERY QUALITY OF INNOVATION and celebration that was represented by the triumphs of Empire, the event was to be publicised and immortalised by the attendance – at the event – of a world-famous photographer. It was the first time that such an exciting prospect had been initiated on this scale, and others have followed suit, including nowadays at the Academy Awards. In 2013, the celebrated celebrity photographer Mark Seliger was approached by *Vanity Fair* magazine with the proposal to set up a backstage studio, a photobooth at their famous Oscars party, where selected stars could sit for a portrait. Rather than submit to the lottery of quick snaps over which they had no control, celebrities could sit with their carefully curated costume to be captured by a professional who would ensure that their image could be crafted to best advantage. It was such a success that stars have been immortalised in this way for the past decade. The *Vanity Fair* Oscars Party has become as famous as the global celebration itself, and just as in 1897, celebrities are captured in their finery through tantalising photographs of fabulous over-the-top outfits.

The Duchess of Devonshire had commissioned a full studio to be built within a marquee in the enormous garden. Props and backdrops were placed at the disposal of the guests. It was a tremendous coup for the photographic firm Lafayette. Despite its name, this firm was not in any way French – the name had been selected by the Irishman James Stack Lauder, the eldest son of the talented photographer Edmund Lauder, who had successfully opened a daguerreotype studio in Dublin in 1853. Four of his sons had followed him into the business. In choosing to change the name, twenty-seven-year-old James wished to capitalise on the fashion for all things French: Paris was a renowned centre of the world of arts and he had studied there.

The new direction built on the success of the three studios run by Edmund, and soon the four brothers – all experienced photographers – were known as running the finest portrait studio in Ireland. There were favoured commissions from the Viceroy and leading members of the Anglo-

Irish aristocracy.[76] By 1884 the firm was securely in the limelight, winning favourable reviews and prizes. James Lafayette (as he was now known) was elected to the Photographic Society of Great Britain, and in 1885 the studio came to the notice of the royal family with its extremely popular portraits of Princess Alexandra on the occasion of her Royal Visit to Ireland. In 1887 his fortune was assured when he was invited to Windsor to photograph the Queen; the Royal Warrant that followed sealed his success.

Business had expanded rapidly, as technology improved and the appetite for quality photographs produced in the proliferation of magazines and newspapers increased through seemingly insatiable public demand. The 'Photographer Royal' was the obvious choice for the prestigious Devonshire House Ball. The Duchess of Devonshire would provide her guests with the opportunity to preserve their fantastic costumes and memories for years to come. The studio at the ball was such a roaring success that many guests made appointments to be photographed in the Bond Street studio if they could not be accommodated on the night. James Lauder and his brothers became the most famous photographers of their time. After the great event, their studio was filled for years thereafter with famous society figures, royals, and the most prominent people of the day.

The development of the press, along with the technological advances in the field of photography (speeding up the exposure process considerably, far more comfortable for the sitter) combined with the thrill for the growing middle classes of celebrity-seeking to create a thriving market for portraits. Other studios proliferated, as the possibilities of purchasing portraits of the royals or the good-looking upper-class women known as 'Professional Beauties' increased. Most middle-class households were proud to display postcard pictures available at competitive rates from their local newsagents or small shops.

Furthermore, portraits became available to the less well-off. Only the very wealthy could afford to commission a painting, but large numbers could, and did, choose to preserve themselves for posterity by posing for a photograph in one of the many specialist studios. All the major towns and cities had at least one such studio, and families had studio stills taken to commemorate births, weddings and other significant moments. Individuals were posed on their own, or in selected groups. There is an abiding fascination in placing an image to a person, as all of us with family photographs can attest.

The idea, however, of preserving a special moment in time, in real time, was a novel one – and added a piquancy and freshness to the Devonshire House Ball. It also added a triumphant element to the Jubilee. An extraordinarily astute political hostess, Louise believed that she was performing her patriotic duty to the Empire by visibly promoting Britain's glorious past, present and future with a celebration that would be sought-after and remembered. The Ball would be associated with the nation's greatness, and the nation's greatest must be represented. Thus, the cream of the political, diplomatic – domestic and foreign – aristocratic and financial worlds would be invited.

To ensure attendance, and splendour, the concept of photographing the costumes was a stroke of genius. James Lafayette, accustomed to capturing the royal family and other high-ranking members of society, was a habitual proponent of props. In much the same way as the famed Dutch portraitists used props to send coded messages in their paintings, Lafayette used objects to exemplify and amplify his sitter's visual representation. The backdrops, lighting, plants, swords, spears and other materials were assembled in the large studio at the Ball, and guests queued for their turn.

It was too big a task to photograph the large number of the 700 guests who wanted their picture taken in character and in their outfits. The society photographers Bassano, Alice Hughes, J. Thomson, Henry Van der Weyde and a few others were also called upon. As planned, a book was commissioned by the Duchess of Devonshire's Committee to present to the Duchess. The photogravures were prepared and fifty copies were printed by the firm Walker & Boutall in 1899. There are a very few copies remaining and the pictures are magnificent, beautifully detailed.

The portraits look remarkably like those of the most celebrated portrait artists of the day, notably the most renowned, John Singer Sargent. The American painter – born in Florence – had trained in Paris before moving to London. After his coup in displaying the controversial *Portrait of Madame X* in Paris in 1884,[77] he relocated after the scandal to Britain, where he soon became the leading portrait painter of his time. For over twenty years, he produced magnificent pictures of the moneyed classes and famous figures of the period. He was not the only sought-after portraitist, but his creations – notably of beautiful women, beautifully dressed and with an immaculate strength of presence – reigned supreme. The men were just as beautiful: Joseph Chamberlain is immortalised hard at work, leaning on a stack of official papers, 'his orchid the only splash of colour between his high starched collar and the flash of cuff under his long, black frock coat'.[78]

Sargent's portraits of figures in elaborate stylised costume with props – often selected by the artist himself – proved useful templates for guests choosing their outfits and overall style. Others toured the galleries and sourced portraits by the Dutch masters, in particular, for both inspiration and copying. Some costumes replicated such historical portraits in every faithful detail. Many felt that their participation in the Jubilee Ball was a tribute to the importance of the occasion, and an opportunity not just for amusement (although that was clearly a great incentive) but to visibly display patriotism, and loyalty to the Crown.

Other senior and well-connected supporters of Empire – political, cultural and economic – were also called on to support the Jubilee by hosting events, investing in the celebrations and, of course, attending the manifestations of imperial glamour and might. Lord Lansdowne, serving as Secretary of State for War, hosted parties at the magnificent Lansdowne House (recently vacated from its tenancy by William Waldorf Astor in early 1896), including one for Indian military officers. A very wealthy Anglo-Irish Protestant, with large properties in Ireland – he played a significant role as a senior Liberal Unionist and Empire enthusiast (he had served as Governor-General of Canada, 1883–88) – Lansdowne hosted a very large dinner for the Prince and Princess of Wales, along with foreign envoys, a week prior to the Devonshire House extravaganza.[79] He attended the Ball as Prince Kaunitz, part of the retinue of Empress Maria Theresa, headed by that formidable wielder of soft power, political hostess Lady Londonderry.

The Prince of Wales played a dominant role in making the Ball a success. Even though Bertie was a political lightweight through circumstance, he was heir to the throne, and an enormously important social arbiter. Indeed, the heir was not, as was often believed, 'politically negligible': through the avenues of 'his clubs and his circle of "fast" playmates, he made his views known and sometimes took it upon himself to lecture cabinet ministers about their failure of strategy or resolution'.[80] The Prince wanted a splendid marking of the Jubilee, perhaps to try to please his notoriously unpleasable mother, or perhaps to visibly and publicly consolidate his status as King in Waiting in a magnificent, showy way. He wanted it – and thus, it was important.

The Prince was very friendly with the Duchess of Devonshire – they both loved gambling over card games – and he was of course to be the star guest at the Ball, with his wife Alexandra. The interest the ball stimulated, and the dramatic impact of the press reportage and the photographs generated, created a sensation. The curiosity of seeing and being seen is a very interesting aspect of Victorian culture. The technology and subsequent desire to be captured by a lens created not just an industry but contributed to a society where appearance became translated into an identity separate from inhabiting the present. It enabled individuals to see how others saw them, and it provided a means whereby projecting one's own identity could become a matter of personal choice. The many posed, stilted pictures that we see can portray stiff, unbending images but can also at times show us people as they wanted to be seen. It was the beginning of the 'selfie', with huge implications that have shaped and formed society in profound ways.

The imitation game was good for business, making it good for Britain. The ruling elite recognised and acknowledged the implicit bargain between their overwhelming privilege and their duty and obligation to organise, and to participate in social events. There was a clear obligation to support visibly – by funds and their presence – community and charitable

HIH The Grand Duke Michael of Russia as Henri IV
The Countess Torby as Gabrielle d'Estrées

causes. This privileged group also understood that the nation's continued economic and political success was largely dependent upon social access between individuals in government and the socially elite – whose status was typically founded on land and lineage. The role of the great political hostesses such as Louise, Duchess of Devonshire, facilitated this, by hosting country house weekends and lavish entertainments. Indeed, she was known contemporaneously as 'the most powerful person outside the government'.[81]

V

THE PLAYERS

The historic and fancy-dress ball given by the Duchess of Devonshire at Devonshire House, and attended by many members of the Royal Family and their distinguished guests, besides the flower of our English aristocracy, was one of unparalleled magnificence and splendour.[82]

FOREIGN RELATIONS:
HARTY-TARTY AND THE DOUBLE DUCHESS
(THE DUKE AND DUCHESS OF DEVONSHIRE)

LOUISE, DUCHESS OF DEVONSHIRE, WAS ONE OF THE UNDISPUTED queens of Victorian society. A German aristocrat by birth, she had accomplished the extraordinary feat of marrying not one but two British dukes. At the age of twenty, in 1852, Luise (later anglicised to Louise) Friedericke Auguste von Alten married William Drogo Montagu (then Viscount Mandeville) in Hanover, and they went on to have two sons and three daughters. Life with Mandeville was challenging: like many of his forebears (and descendants), the young aristocrat had issues with money. The classic attractions for wealthy unemployed upper-class men of gambling and pursuing unsuitable women were epitomised by this rather indolent man. Mandeville had fathered an illegitimate child in 1850; the young woman was married off by the family.

Undeterred by her husband's lack of ambition, Louise pursued her aims to hold an important social position in her adoptive country. Her English was excellent; she had had an English governess, and her family had long been connected to Britain. Louise's great-uncle Ernest von Alten had served with distinction under Wellington in the Peninsular War while Hanover was under Napoleonic domination, and he had distinguished himself at the command of the Hanoverian troops at Waterloo. The Hanoverian court had close links with England, and the Altens were one of the most prominent families there. General von Alten was a Knight of the Bath, and was the representative of the court at the coronation of Queen Victoria.[83]

The family was very wealthy, with a castle and a town house, and all five children – four girls and one boy – were well educated. The Altens travelled to the Riviera, and Louise, the family beauty at age twenty, apparently caught the eye of the Viscount in Nice, a popular watering hole for the upper classes during the winter months. Mandeville was the eldest son of the 6th Duke of Manchester. His expected succession to the title was certainly a large part of his appeal; at the age of twenty-nine, of unattractive appearance, he had retired from ten years in the Guards to take a safe seat in Parliament without any apparent ambition. The couple were frequently short of money. The Manchester family owned an estate at Tandragee[84] in County Armagh in Ireland, where the young couple spent time (often banished for spending too much money) after their marriage. In Ireland, Louise set about her duties with aplomb, teaching the local children and visiting the sick.

On a visit to Paris, where the Manchesters were received by Napoleon III, Louise made her usual strong impression on the British Ambassador, Lord Cowley. Her friends remarked on how much she enjoyed her visits to the French court. The pleasure-loving Emperor and Empress and their entourage encouraged Louise in gambling and other sybaritic activities – she enjoyed them enormously, but also built up a store of amusing anecdotes with which she entertained acquaintances for years to come.

Louise pursued her ambitions with what she had: an appetite for power, a drive to succeed, good looks and a charming manner. At age twenty-six, in February 1859, she was made Mistress of the Robes, a political appointment secured for her through the intervention of Lord Derby, who had found her very charming. Victoria had discovered in her a pleasant companion, but the fall of Lord Derby's ministry the following year led to her dismissal. Her social gains with the Queen were considerably diluted, however, over the following few years thanks to her adoption of a 'fast' lifestyle in the set of the party-loving Prince of Wales. Louise was, pointedly, not invited to Bertie's wedding to Alexandra in 1863. Her friendship with the Prince deepened nevertheless – they shared a passion for gambling and for following the races.

Although the Mandevilles – later Manchesters – were not a compatible couple, they did produce five children in rapid succession, between 1853 and 1862. They drifted apart, however, and soon lived quite independent lives. Neither was faithful. Louise engaged in a number of relationships with admiring young men; her beauty struck those who met her when she came to England after her marriage. In a society that revered beauty, Louise stood out, and made the most of her looks. The Queen wrote to her daughter, Victoria, Princess Royal, that she had seen Louise on one of her first appearances: she was 'very smart and looked very pretty'.[85] Even years later, in 1873 when Louise was over forty, the Polish-Russian aristocrat and author Princess Catherine Radziwill recorded: 'She struck me as the loveliest creature I had ever set my eyes upon. Indeed, I have only met in my whole existence three women who could be compared to her.'[86]

Despite an affiliation through her husband to the Tory party, the young Duchess made the important conquest of the Liberal politician Lord Cowper (who later became Lord Lieutenant of Ireland, 1880–82); in the 1850s he became a frequent visitor to the family seat at Kimbolton at Huntingdonshire. Mandeville inherited the ducal title and Kimbolton in 1855, and the Duke and Duchess of Manchester travelled between their homes in the country, in Ireland, their London house and the French Riviera. Manchester, a man of so little promise, fulfilled his destiny by becoming a society bore, a man of meagre achievement and decidedly odd ideas, attending military manoeuvres and passing comment, despite having no expertise. He was notoriously hopeless with money, and soon the estates were mortgaged.

Manchester was sufficiently canny, however, to contrive the award of a series of honours, one of which was an invitation in 1858 to join a group attempting to revive the Knights Hospitaller of St John (also known as the Order of St John), a medieval Christian military order founded in the eleventh century, originally to care for sick pilgrims in Jerusalem. It had then developed into a military order during the Crusades and played an important part in defending the Holy Land, becoming over time a large and powerful military and naval organisation; it exists today as the Sovereign Military Order of Malta. The Order of St John remained focused on humanitarian and charitable works; its revival in Britain began in the mid-1830s, and it became affiliated with the St John Ambulance Brigade, which continues its humanitarian work globally.

But Manchester's good works, such as they were, did not define his life as much as did his love of gambling and lavish spending. There were periodic crises when finances became precarious, and by the time of his death, a number of properties had had to be sold. The Duke, suffering the many health problems associated with dissolute living, was frequently ill. He died at the age of sixty-seven at the Hotel Royal in Naples. Louise managed – just – to be by his bedside the night before he died, having travelled to Naples from Monte Carlo. Manchester had been ill with dysentery and peritonitis, although his doctor had hoped that he might recover. Their eldest son was a bankrupt, and in disgrace, and the younger son did not arrive in time for his father's death. Manchester's body was embalmed and returned to England to be buried.

The eldest son, now Viscount Mandeville, was entirely unsatisfactory. Upon the death of his father, newspaper commentary referred to the young man as having a name that has 'unhappily been familiar to newspaper readers for a year or two past'.[87] Other newspapers were more explicit, stating that the new Lord Mandeville's was a name 'not altogether unknown in music-hall circles'.[88] Mandeville was notorious for his love of showgirls, despite having married the Cuban-American Consuelo Yznaga in 1876. In a curious twist, Consuelo, as we will see, became one of Bertie's intimates, despite frosty relations with her mother-in-law, the Prince's great friend.

The Duchess, Louise, began her famous liaison with Spencer Compton Cavendish, Marquess of Hartington, in the early 1860s. After a long-

The Countess of Mar and Kellie as Dante's Beatrice

standing affair with the courtesan known as 'Skittles', Hartington had become involved with Louise (rumour has it that Louise made sure her rival was firmly despatched by encouraging her lover to take a well-timed trip to America). The affair presumably began after the birth of Louise's last child in 1862, and was a somewhat open secret in political circles, never revealed publicly for fear of hurting Hartington's political prospects. He and Louise addressed one another formally in public, and he even accompanied the Manchesters on trips abroad. One of the consequences of Louise maintaining a separate lifestyle while conducting a clandestine affair over a thirty-year period (Manchester did not die until 1890) was that the Duke of Devonshire had no heir. The secrecy needed to maintain the relationship, furthermore, reinforced the habits of a lonely childhood and Hartington had a well-merited reputation for aloofness.

He was not, however, lacking in a sense of humour. Benjamin Disraeli – who liked him – reported a conversation between Hartington and the Austrian Ambassador, at which the Ambassador had commented that 'what with whist, the turf, &, what I delicately called "morning visits" [to the Duchess], I wonder how you can find time for politics', and Hartington had smoothly replied, 'I wonder too.'[89]

Manchester had played to perfection the role of the disinterested husband, often accompanying his wife and her lover on trips to France. The liaison between the Duchess of Manchester and Hartington was kept under wraps with the delicacy reserved for the discreet affairs of the upper class. Although it seems quite incredible to imagine now, in the age of transparency on social media and elsewhere, the secret was kept because the couple never demonstrated any strong emotion to one another in public. But politicians soon understood that in dealing with Hartington they had to reckon with Louise, who increasingly acted as his political hostess and most important confidante. For the Queen's Golden Jubilee, in 1887, Louise hosted a royal fete at Crystal Palace, which Sir Edward Hamilton described as including Randolph Churchill and 'Masher' Joe Chamberlain. There had been a concert, followed by a walk in the garden and a 'scrambling dinner' – after which the party had watched fireworks.[90] A fortnight later, the indefatigable Louise hosted another party, where 'in one room Princess Alexandra was dancing "with inimitable grace"; in another the Prince and a group of gilded youths were at baccarat and Chamberlain playing with them for high stakes while Randolph Churchill kept the bank'.[91]

Extraordinarily wealthy (despite regular complaints about rising maintenance costs on his estates, and taxation and diminishing income), supremely disinterested and notoriously lazy, Hartington was a reluctant, albeit dedicated, politician who was happiest indulging his love of the turf. Despite this, he became a successful senior Liberal statesman for many years – and famously turned down the premiership three times, each time for various reasons, in 1880, 1886 and 1887. He had a reputation for fairmindedness and independence of thought, serving as Irish Secretary, Liberal leader, and later, Secretary for India, and for War, and then as the most senior Liberal Unionist. Hartington, who lived until he was fifty-eight on an allowance from his father, inherited the dukedom in December 1891 and then became one of the wealthiest men in England.

He was a statesman who, in spite of a deliberately cultivated indolent air – and his reputation for laziness – gave a lifetime of service to the nation. A keen member for many years in his natural home of the Liberal Party, his objection to Home Rule, as we have seen, caused him in 1886 to dramatically leave the Liberals and take on the leadership of the newly created Liberal Unionist Party. He became increasingly drawn to policies articulated by the Conservatives and over time, served in Conservative administrations.

His career has been more remembered for his role in bringing down Gladstone, twice, over Home Rule, and for his conflict with imperialists through his own support of free trade, but in his time he was considered the most senior and reliable of British politicians, both in the House of Commons and in the Lords. He was a steadying hand, and highly regarded as a safe influence on the government, capable of making decisions that did not depend on his own personal gain or interest. With the reputation of an honest broker, he was sought after when sensible advice was needed. The Prince of Wales, and later as King, relied on his friend Hartington to resolve problems 'both in matters of a more public character and in private affairs relating to the social world'. Hartington once commented that he didn't know why, 'but whenever a man is caught cheating at cards the case is referred to me'.[92]

A man who would have preferred to spend his time raising racehorses and following them on the track, playing bridge or shooting on one of his estates, he did not shirk his responsibilities and in Louise he found a partner who galvanised him, networked constantly on his behalf and strove to play her part as half of one of the most important couples in Britain. She and Hartington waited a seemly two-year period to marry in August 1892 and from that moment Louise reigned supreme.

She was known for her iron will and determination – driving Hartington to use their exhaustive network to good purpose. Daisy recalled that the Duchess 'never relaxed, never revealed any emotion', appearing 'neither angry nor pleased nor vexed, though at times she would be strident, emphatic and persistent'. Her abilities as a hostess were undeniable: 'she was correct, cordial upon occasion, outspoken, but always unperturbed'. The only time there had been a visible crack in the façade was on an occasion when the Duke had been delayed at Chatsworth after a day's hunting. Louise had stridden restlessly and with 'tears in her eyes' until his safe return. Daisy concluded that although the pair were 'not prepossessing people', their clear 'love for one another was a very beautiful thing'.[93]

The Devonshires and members of other noble families continued to play important roles, especially as Victoria continued to shun society, upholding the mourning and social withdrawal she had entered into upon the death of Albert. Bertie was only too delighted to have in Louise a wealthy fellow aficionada of gambling – on the turf and at the card table. Entertainments at the Duke's magnificent homes at Chatsworth and in Devonshire House in London were highly coveted invitations, and Louise ruled high society with an iron fist. The Devonshires were especially assiduous in developing and using their homes as venues for political activity and lobbying.

Some of Hartington's complaints about costs did have some merit. It was clear, by the end of the century, that the great landed estates were vulnerable to the decreasing rent revenues and increasing costs of retaining tenants and workers. In fact, these large properties were 'most affected by the gross economic and political changes at the end of the century because they were as likely to be symbols of aristocratic wealth and privilege as of art or history. Places such as Chatsworth, Blenheim, Belvoir and Eaton were very ostentatious and very expensive to keep up, thus difficult for both owners and public.'[94]

The 8th Duke was, however, as we have seen, one of the wealthiest men in the land. His life had not been altogether an easy one, though. His mother had died when he was just seven years old, and he and his two younger brothers were educated at home by their father, who was very learned but known as a serious, devout man. Known at first as Lord Cavendish, Hartington had been brought up in an isolated, withdrawn atmosphere until he attended Trinity College, Cambridge, where he took a second-class degree without undue effort. He did little but lead the life of an upper-class aristocrat until he was persuaded to take a safe parliamentary seat as a Liberal in 1857. Upon the death of the 6th Duke the following year, when his father succeeded to the dukedom and estates as the 7th Duke, he became Marquess of Hartington – the name by which he became most commonly known and one that was shortened, in political circles, to Harty or even Harty-Tarty.

Hartington[95] remained, as we have seen, financially dependent on his father until he was fifty-eight years of age, receiving an allowance and regular settlement of his debts. His father disapproved of his eldest son's passion for the turf – which was so pronounced that the heir built himself a house near the racing at Newmarket. He spent vast sums on his hobby, with varying degrees of success – and he enjoyed, too, shooting, and bridge, which he played into the night at one of his clubs. His self-contained, unemotional manner, however, concealed a devotion to politics that few would have suspected from his rather abstract demeanour. Hartington was soon identified by Liberal leaders as a man of promise and flew through the ranks to senior positions in government.

When Gladstone was defeated at the general election of 1874 – and later resigned as Liberal leader in the Commons – Hartington was elected, rather against his will, as his successor. Despite this initial hesitation, he mastered this new post with quiet, hard work and an unswerving dedication to traditional, conservative values. He never became Prime Minister – mainly because Gladstone returned to the fold, and also, it must be said, because of a natural diffidence and one might say the lack of an identifiable political platform upon which to drive a premiership.

Instead, the role of highly influential elder statesman probably became him most, largely because he had actually gained experience in a number of positions of operational responsibility – including, as we know, the lord-lieutenancy for Ireland, and Secretary of State for India and for War. He split with Gladstone over the Home Rule Bill for Ireland – to which he was bitterly opposed – and thenceforth led a dissident group of Liberal Unionists, creating a bond with the Conservatives who upheld the Union. This had been a very difficult decision for him to take. Lady Randolph Churchill (Jennie) recalled asking Hartington whether he was prepared to jettison Gladstone and 'join them' to defeat Home Rule, whereupon he had replied that he had 'not yet decided, but when I do, I suppose I shall be thought either a man or a mouse'. Jennie's quick reply of 'or a rat', triggered an angry response from her husband when she told him about it, having, she admitted, thought herself rather clever. She did understand, though, the political challenges of the situation, noting that many of their Liberal friends 'were in great trepidation at that time, torn between their hatred of Home Rule and their reluctance to leave the "Grand Old Man"'.[96]

In 1891 Hartington succeeded to the dukedom and continued his leadership of the Liberal Unionists in the House of Lords. As he was a secretive man by upbringing and nature, Hartington's unusual life was a closed book to any but his closest friends and colleagues because of his unorthodox private arrangement with the Manchesters. Friends and colleagues knew, too, that the Duke was essentially simple and unintellectual in his outlook, despite his enormous privilege; cultural and social life was to be borne, rather than enjoyed. As the historian Peter Mandler observed, by the 1890s:

The Countess of Westmorland as Hebe

The slow stripping of the country houses, and the build-up of the great American collections amongst others, had begun. The eighth Duke of Devonshire, as Lord Hartington the last of the great Whig politicians, bored with everything except racehorses and the Duchess of Manchester, his mistress, was typical in his ignorance. One of the duties of the Chatsworth librarian was to 'tour the principal rooms with the Eighth Duke and his Duchess the day before a house-party began, and tell them a few outstanding facts about their principal possessions'.[97]

Hartington may have found it difficult to interest himself in his possessions, but he fought hard to keep them, and the inherited estates, intact for future generations. Evidence presented by Cannadine demonstrates the Duke's clever and focused approach to reducing costs and streamlining inefficient operations run by the Devonshire estate.[98] Previous investments made by the 7th Duke outside agriculture had proved disastrous and had to be remedied. Those who worked with him observed that the 8th Duke, 'when he did start to work', was 'untiring and had a shrewd intelligence and a retentive memory'.[99] It is further proof of Hartington's desire to make Louise happy that he subsidised the very expensive entertaining that meant so much to her.

Indeed, for the 8th Duchess, social engagement was her lifeblood, and she was exceedingly skilled at the politics of relationships. Like all talented networkers, she actually enjoyed the cut and thrust of social tactics and channelled her intelligence, considerable energy and talents into achieving the domination of her set. In this she was helped – as she had been in her youth – by her great beauty. It was, after all, a young Louise, with a perfect profile and magnificent features and figure, who had captured the young Montagu.

With her genius for entertaining, honed after years of practice as Hartington's top and most trusted confidante, she had the knack of putting together people who might not be inclined to mix socially, but who could be persuaded to become political allies. As Lady Mandeville, she had used her charms on many willing admirers, and managed, with some assiduity, to lead Bertie's Marlborough House set and to regain her good terms with the Queen. Nevertheless, Victoria urged the Princess of Wales to drop the Duchess, in disapproval of her racy style.

After marriage to Hartington, however, Louise was a frequent guest of the Queen, dining regularly at Osborne House. There was no stopping her ambitions after 1892, when she assumed the crown of high society. Lavish and spectacular entertainments were her trademark, and she took her political responsibilities very seriously. Receptions at Devonshire House and at the magnificent country house at Chatsworth were renowned for their extravagance and opulence. Despite Hartington's reservations about income, there was no stinting in entertaining.

Parties at their country estate at Chatsworth could, according to one guest, include as many as '470 people' who, along with the staff, 'would be put up in the house, and everything was on a corresponding style of lavish display'.[100] Augusta Fane claimed that anyone of those 'who worked by the day was allowed to take away sufficient food for his supper'. The custom had had to be stopped, however, 'as non-workers came from near and far for a free meal, and one man was seen to remove his supper in a wheelbarrow!'[101] As we can see, the Duke and Duchess were literally running a medium-sized company, with large numbers of employees and huge supply chains (with concomitant waste). Hartington had no interest in this side of his life, but Louise took it on with gusto.

A woman of formidable organisational talents, she was clever and not only helped her husband in his political work, but in running the enterprise that was his life. She provides an excellent example of a woman denied the political sphere herself, using every opportunity to exercise soft power and influence – behaviours that are replicated today by royals and diplomats all over the globe. The couple, in their later years, hosted regular parties in their homes, mostly involving some kind of card game and outdoor pursuits. The Duke spent a great deal of time sorting out his finances; regular high expenditures had to be investigated and many extravagances identified and tidied up.[102] The costs of Louise's great parties were borne, and they served as punctuation points of the season. The Ball of 1897 was essentially an occasion of state, and she saw herself as an integral part of the highest pinnacle of society.

On the night of her Ball, she had, fittingly, posed like the Sun Queen at the summit of the famed curved crystal staircase of Devonshire House. Together, the Double Duchess and Harty-Tarty – as the senior Liberal statesman continued to be known – literally towered over the nation's social and political elite. Louise was bedecked by the famed Devonshire diamonds, and her silk gown – designed by the famed French couturier Worth – was wrought in star-like designs and featured outstretched peacock tails that were outlined in precious gems reflecting the shimmering light. As Zenobia, Queen of Palmyra, she stood, poised and self-assured, adorned by her regal train of green velvet, intricately hand-embroidered in Eastern designs, with a lotus flower motif in rubies, sapphires and emeralds. This was the apogee of her triumph, of the long journey from Hanover and first marriage to a flawed man to an undisputed position of leadership, beside the man she loved.

KING ARTHUR AND 'OUR JOE': ARTHUR BALFOUR AND JOSEPH CHAMBERLAIN

As we have seen, one of the primary purposes of the Devonshire House Ball was to present an event which publicly portrayed a unified political – and social – front. This was possible in part because there had been a number of political and economic developments that had brought about unprecedented cooperation between individuals, and even provoked a marked departure from traditional party lines for certain people. The friendly relations between two fellow guests – the notoriously aloof, languid aristocrat Arthur Balfour (*see page 15*) (his godfather and namesake was the Duke of Wellington) and the brash, dynamic industrialist Joseph Chamberlain – exemplified this bringing together of unexpected bedfellows: two men of very different backgrounds, ideals and political vision.

Traditionally, social entertaining among the elite had taken place along loosely defined party lines. Liberal proposals for Home Rule and the ensuing fallout over the Irish Question had caused such cataclysmic ill-will, however, that individuals sought to overcome this impediment to friendship by creating different social sets, of which one of the most famous was 'The Gang', later known as 'The Souls'. Further, the hitherto unknown phenomenon of two courts had opened the door to competing social groups, some of which had evolved in response to the other. The Souls had developed in large part thanks to an antipathy to the 'court' of the Prince of Wales and his Marlborough House set (named after his residence), which they considered shallow and showy.

The Souls took pride in being intellectual, witty, sensitive (hence their nickname) and given to deep friendships between the sexes that were either sexual or platonic (or, sometimes, serially both). They considered themselves the antithesis – although there was considerable overlap – to the racy, fast-living, gambling Marlborough House set. Arthur Balfour was 'king' of this privileged group, and the links between the members were evident as much in politics as in the drawing room.

George Curzon (soon to become Viceroy of India), for example, was a founder member of this elite social group, which was originally made up of the aristocratic families of Balfours, Lyttletons, Tennants and Wyndhams. They were later joined by the Charteris and Manners families and a few others. Held together by friendships, marriages, affairs and politics, the group grew as relationships and affiliations developed. Led by Balfour ('King Arthur'), the set rejected being grouped with other social cliques of the time, preferring rounds of golf and literary discussions to bridge and hunting, and opening membership up beyond aristocratic circles.

The Souls were enormously privileged by birth and by their wealth. In spite of their pretensions to elevated 'souls', they did not take themselves lightly as a rule. One 'friend' suggested that Margot Asquith's (*see page 57*) book, *Memoirs*, should have been called *The Importance of Being Margot*,[103] and this does rather neatly sum up how some of 'The Gang' came across. As members of some of the nation's most prominent families, many were present at the Ball. St-John Brodrick; Hugo Charteris, Lord Elcho; Mary

Charteris, Lady Elcho; Alfred Lyttleton; Percy Wyndham; Madeline Wyndham; George Wyndham; William Grenfell, 1st Baron Desborough; Ethel, 'Ettie', Lady Desborough; Henry White, the US diplomat, and, later, his wife Margaret; Violet Manners, Duchess of Rutland, amid others prepared their costumes assiduously, and many chose to perform at the Ball as members of one of the courts.

Arthur Balfour was, perhaps, a reluctant participant. His renowned good looks – Beatrice Webb, a hard-headed socialist and economist, described him as 'a charming person. Tall, good-looking, and intellectual'[104] – along with his impeccable lineage, opened all doors to him and he was invited everywhere, especially welcome as an eligible single man. Yet he was at heart a solitary creature and endowed with a natural elegance that precluded making a fool of himself in public. And he had an elevated political position to maintain.

He was, from 1892, Leader of the House of Commons. His approach to the job was underlaid with the sensitivity that comes of personal tragedy and loss. Although Balfour's background had been one of great privilege, his father had died while Arthur was a young boy, leaving his bereft widow to raise eight children. Despite her immense grief, she, a deeply devout woman, fiercely instilled in them a great drive to please her, and to be successful. This suited some of the siblings: Arthur, of course, ultimately achieved the highest office of the land as Prime Minister; his brother Frank, an eminent scientist, had a professorial chair created for him at Cambridge, where his sister Eleanor was Principal of Newnham College, while their brother Gerald achieved the political heights of a Cabinet position.[105]

Arthur had been left a wealthy man after his father's death, and grew up at the impressive 10,000-acre estate at Whittinghame in East Lothian. The children were taught by their mother, however, to appreciate their good fortune and to take nothing for granted. They were all set to do housework in order to help offset staff losses during the cotton depression in 1862. Although the life was one of economic security and high social status, they did not escape the miseries of frequent illness caused by a rude climate, and Arthur was felt to be a 'delicate' child, often unwell and far

Lord Rodney as King Arthur of the Round Table

from robust physically. This languor became a permanent feature of his life, with friends and colleagues often observing 'the exhausted exterior presented to the world'.[106] His desire to conserve his energy gave him a long life, but may have accounted for a certain lack of concerted drive to achieve his full potential.

He followed the traditionally elite path of Eton, then Trinity College, Cambridge, where he took a degree in moral sciences. Balfour took to society with elan: wonderfully well connected, he was an immediate success and much sought-after. His uncle was the political and territorial magnate Lord Salisbury, and visits to the magnificent Hatfield had impressed the Balfour clan throughout Arthur's childhood. In 1870 Balfour himself purchased a large house in London's fashionable and expensive Carlton Gardens. The mansion was close to that of the Gladstone family, with whom Balfour maintained a strong friendship begun in his childhood.

Where Balfour had benefited from an aristocratic – albeit not entirely rosy – background of inherited privilege, Chamberlain's roots were solidly in the industrial class. His ancestors, rural in origin, were involved in small businesses rather than farming, and one of Joseph's grandfathers, Henry, had migrated to London, where Joseph's father had met his wife, Caroline. She came from a family that had once been quite well off, and was a strict disciplinarian who insisted that her children be brought up to write beautifully and to speak well. It was a huge gift to her eight living children, and provided Joseph, the eldest, with a solid education and confidence in his intellectual abilities.

Their London home was one of relative affluence, of City people with rational Unitarian beliefs. The Chamberlains hosted many jolly family gatherings, where spirits ran high and everyone enjoyed putting on plays: 'Young Joe threw himself into these private theatricals with gusto, eventually becoming the chief producer and taking the exaggerated character parts.'[107] This talent for drama was to serve him well in the House of Commons and, despite his modest background, Chamberlain presented a sufficiently gentlemanly countenance to be considered 'clubbable', although he was always an outsider, a proud self-made man.

He was an excellent student, ending up at the prestigious University College School, where many well-off Unitarian families sent their sons. Joseph had a huge appetite for learning, and excelled at his subjects, taking prizes in mathematics, Latin and French. During holidays, he satisfied his immense curiosity in science by visiting exhibits of new technology and attending lectures in chemistry, electricity and literature at the Polytechnic Institution.[108] In a nation that idolised sporting prowess, he was completely uninterested in physical pursuits. There was a drive to young Joseph, a strong hunger for success and impact, that characterised the ambition of Britain's rising industrial class.

Balfour, on the other hand, was in no rush to make his mark. He had followed his uncle, Salisbury, to the Conservatives – thus disappointing his friend and earlier mentor, Gladstone. Although Balfour was successful in gaining his seat in 1879, his party was discouraged, and the young politician, aged thirty-two, joined with three backbenchers – including the firebrand Lord Randolph Churchill – to form the Fourth Party (distinct from the Conservatives, Liberals or Irish Nationalists). Although the aspiring politician had not at first been taken very seriously – known as a dreamer, a poet and an accomplished philosopher – he made a success of his position as private secretary in 1878 to Lord Salisbury, then as Foreign Secretary in the Conservative government of Benjamin Disraeli (Lord Beaconsfield). Through the Fourth Party he caused political damage during Gladstone's second premiership, from 1880 to 1885, which culminated in bringing down Gladstone's premiership over the contentious question of Home Rule for Ireland.

On the night of the Ball, Balfour dined with his set, at the home of Lord and Lady Cowper in St James's Square. Many of the 'Souls' were at this event, and although he was very much amongst friends, Edith Chaplin – who was to become the Marchioness of Londonderry – recalled that they were very crowded and her long hair kept falling into his soup. It was a loud and public event, and probably not to his quite austere and refined taste. The Duke of Portland later wrote that Balfour, dressed as a seventeenth-century Dutch nobleman, had 'arrived rather late, trying to creep along the wall behind everyone else'.[109]

Joseph Chamberlain had joined Gladstone's Liberal Party and was appointed President of the Board of Trade in 1880 after a very successful business career. Born and bred in London, he had moved at the age of eighteen to Birmingham to run the screw-making factory founded by his uncle – and was known affectionately in Birmingham as 'Our Joe' after serving as Mayor, 1873–76. He was elected Radical Liberal MP for the city in 1876, and his strong views on free trade and social reform were founded on his commercial experience, which he carried into his political life. He was not an assiduous, smooth-tongued politician, but far more direct. Jennie Churchill recalled how, in 1887, on the occasion of a cruise on a White Star ship to view the naval review for the Queen's Jubilee, Chamberlain had approached Hartington to convince him of the benefits of joining the newly formed National Party. Although plenty of political discussion had taken place among the guests, Jennie observed with dismay (her husband Randolph was very keen to get Hartington's support for the venture) that Chamberlain drew up a chair, and 'suddenly plunged into the matter without preliminaries and with his usual directness'.[110]

Despite Hartington's obvious discomfiture, Chamberlain, 'full of his scheme, pressed the points home, taking no notice of the monosyllables he got in answer'. The conversation eventually 'languished' and the subject, she wrote, 'was never re-opened'.[111] This was but one illustration of the gap between the clever businessman and the high-level politicians with whom he sought to work. This talented businessman was able to bring to his political vision an understanding of the life of the working man in a way that traditional aristocrats such as Balfour simply could not.

Chamberlain made a strong impact early on, and Prime Minister Gladstone appointed him to the Cabinet, as President of the Board of Trade, in 1880. He was deeply committed to Empire, firmly believing in the mutual benefits of imperialism; he was, too, deeply committed to maintaining good relationships with the colonies. Chamberlain became personally involved with the problems created by the agitation and unrest in Ireland. Trying to resolve the 'Irish Question' became a dominant feature of his politics. Vehemently against independence for Ireland in the form of Home Rule – as was supported by Gladstone – he was nevertheless in favour of local government for the island.

One of the reasons for Chamberlain's success was because men such as he were increasingly relevant to politics at the highest level. As the franchise had been extended, more attention had to be paid to the needs of greater masses of voters, and experienced men of business, like Chamberlain, could speak for the working man. This was increasingly critical for both main political parties: the process of industrialisation had created as one consequence a major population shift from agriculture to industrial towns and cities, and the voting base grew also from expansion: from a base of just under 9 million in 1801 in England and Wales, the population was up to 32.5 million by 1901.

A savvy businessman and assiduous politician, a man such as Chamberlain could hope for great influence and power. As the economic base of the nation shifted in favour of newer forms of wealth creation, there was a concomitant rise in the bestowal of status on high achievers. There had always been those men, or women, who rose through the ranks with talent, good fortune, charm and drive – but it was not really until the late Victorian age that wealth, with a landed estate, was sufficient to obtain membership to high society. Previously, the possession of wealth, land and titles had provided the entrance to the very highest echelons of society. Now, wealth alone (enhanced, preferably, by a landed estate), could serve as introduction – this is because, for the first time, 'non-landed incomes and wealth had begun to overtake land alone as the main source of economic power'.[112]

When Gladstone proposed Home Rule as an integral part of the Liberal position in 1886, Chamberlain, newly appointed as President of the Local Government Board, was so much in disagreement that he resigned from the Cabinet and became leader of the Liberal Unionists, forming an alliance with the Conservatives in opposition to Home Rule. Chamberlain's controversial move also reinforced his changing views on trade, and he became an increasingly forceful proponent of imperial protectionism. After the success of the Conservative–Liberal Unionist coalition in the election of 1895,

Chamberlain was appointed as Secretary of State for the Colonies, where he used his platform and position to support closer ties within the Empire. A keen enthusiast for imperial preference, marked by preferential imperial trade agreements, he was in the vanguard of a strain of populist 'jingoism' that had pervaded national life, especially after the election. Chamberlain believed that the Empire would provide opportunities for all participants to thrive, and that 'a common trade policy is the indispensable basis of a common imperial policy'. He argued forcibly that such a common policy would benefit each constituent unit of the Empire, and that the whole would be in a position 'to safeguard, and promote the development of each'.[113]

The preparation for an election of a coalition government in 1895 had not been smooth. By 1893, there had been growing speculation about changes on the political stage, and the possibilities of such a coalition. Collaboration between parties was, as a general rule, as unwelcome as it is now, and brought many complications in its wake. It was a measure of the difficulties in reconciling profound disagreements on the Irish Question and on the place of free trade that such partnerships had even to be contemplated. There was increasing excitement and guessing in political circles and in the press.

The *Truth* newspaper had excitedly predicted: 'THE DEVONSHIRE–CHAMBERLAIN COALITION'. The story was picked up and reported in other papers: the plan of the Liberal Unionists – should they win the next election – was to form a government headed by the Duke of Devonshire, with Arthur Balfour leading the House of Commons, Lord Salisbury as Foreign Secretary and a suggestion 'that Mr Chamberlain should sit by Mr Balfour as the head of one of the great departments'. Such a plan was, the article continued, 'within the area of practical politics', but the Tories 'would never consent either that Mr Chamberlain should be the Premier of the coalition, or that, while the uncle yields his place to the Duke of Devonshire in the Lords, the nephew should yield his place to Mr Chamberlain in the House of Commons'. The piece concluded on a practical note that this proposed coalition had 'first to catch the bear before the skin was divided'.[114]

Three strong-minded characters, Lord Salisbury, Balfour and

The Duke of Marlborough as the French Ambassador
to the Court of Catherine of Russia

Chamberlain, governed from 1895 until Salisbury's resignation as Premier in 1902. Balfour was considered very useful at keeping in check Chamberlain's vigorous demands for change. Devonshire, as Lord President of the Council, was also a powerful countercheck to too many radical proposals at once. The Colonial Secretary was known for his ruthless personality and was a difficult colleague. His great talent for organising at grassroots level, and for sensing the wider political mood, gave him leverage and he used this power to push his agenda: social reforms, imperial preference and a far more aggressive imperialist strategy than that of his close colleagues. His aggression made life difficult for those such as Balfour who preferred a more collaborative approach and disliked and distrusted confrontation. But Chamberlain, although divisive, was essential. As Winston Churchill later remarked: 'he made the political weather'.[115]

Both Balfour and Chamberlain were guests at the Ball, as were the most significant political figures. Chamberlain attended the Ball dressed as a Louis XVI nobleman. Interestingly, he did not choose to be photographed. Many of his fellow politicians were similarly adorned: former Cabinet and Privy Councillor, Minister Arnold Morley, was a noble gentleman of the Louis XV period; former Prime Minister Lord Rosebery (*see page 51*) attended as Horace Walpole.[116]

For someone like Joe Chamberlain, though, his feelings about the appropriateness of the dressing up were irrelevant. To be included was a clear marker of his elevated social status. The social journey of 'Our Joe' should not be underestimated. His origins were solidly middle-class and his first two marriages had been unremarkable. Harriet Kenrick, his first wife, was the daughter of a hollow-ware manufacturer and died just two years and two children later, in childbirth. A second marriage to Harriet's cousin Florence, with whom he had four children, also ended in tragedy. She too died in childbirth and it was following this second tragedy that Chamberlain lost his personal faith.

His third marriage, in 1888, came as a surprise: he had met the clever, wealthy and very well-connected young American Mary Crowninshield Endicott in New York and had fallen in love. They were soon married and

Mary rapidly became a consummate hostess and an enthusiastic supporter of her husband's career. Her social standing and skills paved the way to ease him into high society in ways that had hitherto been closed to him. 'Our Joe' became a figure relished by cartoonists and artists – his slender, dapper figure graced by his trademark monocle and elegant orchid buttonhole.

Of course, society for the late Victorians, was – like God – English, and not merely English but distinctly aristocratic.[117] In this privileged world of the most elite, it was extraordinarily difficult, as we have seen, for outsiders to penetrate. With few exceptions, Blacks, the Irish, Russians, Jews and those of lower classes – including the modest middle class from which Joseph Chamberlain originated – found the stairs to political prominence or high society access very, very steep. Chamberlain proved the exception to the rule, and his ascent continued through the legacy of his children: two of his sons, Austen and Neville, became as famous as their high-achieving parent.

ROYAL FAVOURITES

Jennie Churchill

DESPITE A REVOLUTION SUCCESSFULLY FOUGHT, one result of which had been the abolition of the Crown – and thus the aristocracy – many wealthy Americans found blue blood in Britain, and on the continent, of considerable appeal. Large cash reserves served in many cases to overcome resistance to Yankee antecedents, traditionally held by families of old lineage. This well-documented transfer of cash for titles grew in importance during the period of Bertie's life as the Prince of Wales. He liked American women, with their winning, forthright ways and rich fathers.

Between 1870 and 1914, there were 104 marriages between British men and American women (some of whom were extremely wealthy and made headlines, though by no means all).[118] There was still, however, considerable entrenched prejudice in the nobility against Americans. It was, for Bertie, a question of money. As we know, he was constantly running short of funds thanks to a passion for gambling and expensive living, and he was quite prepared to open the doors to his well-heeled and charming cousins who had made their home back in the old world. Some social perceptions remained, nevertheless. Lady Augusta Fane – daughter of the 2nd Earl of Stradbrooke – commented in her book published in 1896 that when on a trip to the United States, she had called on a Mr King, Manager of a 'big bank'. He had 'impressed' on her 'to remember that the aristocracy of America was the aristocracy of wealth'.[119]

A number of Bertie's American intimates were guests at the Ball, including Jennie Churchill and her younger sister Leonie Leslie, as well as Consuelo Manchester and her two sisters, Emilie Yznaga and Natica Lister-Kaye. Consuelo Marlborough, of the fabulously wealthy Vanderbilt dynasty, was in attendance, as were Adela Essex and Minnie Paget. Many of these American brides became very popular with a certain set. Florence Williams noted approvingly that they were 'very clever in adapting themselves to all conditions and to the English country-life, which is so different from what they have been accustomed to'; these clever women also 'introduced all sorts of customs from their country, such as bridge, jazz, and cocktails'.[120]

A prominent and clever socialite, Winston's beautiful mother Jennie – daughter of a self-made American millionaire and his snobbish, social-climbing wife – was an enthusiast of costume parties and was thrilled to have a starring role in the Devonshire Ball, thanks to her social position and to her close relationship with Bertie. In her published memoirs (written in 1908 to raise much-needed cash), she described the mounting excitement surrounding the event.

'Great were the confabulations and mysteries', she exclaimed, writing of how with 'bated breath' and 'solemn mien' a guest would 'whisper to some few dozen or more that she was going to represent the Queen of Cyprus or Aspasia, Fredegonde or Petrarch's Laura; but the secret *must* be kept'. There was huge activity, and historical tomes were 'ransacked for inspirations, old pictures and engravings' as attendees became 'quite learned in respect to past celebrities of whom they had never before heard'. Indeed, the obscure was sought after.[121]

Jennie's sharp tongue and observational skills described the discourse beautifully: 'Never heard of Simonetta? How curious! But surely you remember Botticelli's picture of her, one of the beauties of the Florentine Court? No? How strange! [122] 'And: 'My dress is to be "old Venetian" pink velvet, with gold embroideries – one of those medieval women: I can't remember her name, but that's of no consequence. Masses of jewellery, of course.'

She wryly observed that the men were even more competitive about their costumes than the women, adding that there was 'no doubt that when a man begins to think about his appearance he competes with women to some purpose – money, time and thought being of no account to him'. On the night of the Ball itself, there was not a coiffeur or hairdresser to be had, and many were 'so busy' that 'some of the poor victims actually had their locks tortured early in the morning, sitting all day in a rigid attitude….'[123]

On the night itself, Jennie marvelled at the magnificent outfits. Devonshire House was, she claimed, 'with its marble staircase and glorious pictures', the most 'fitting frame for the distinguished company which thronged its beautiful rooms'. She noted approvingly that:

Everyone of note and interest was there, representing the intellect, beauty and fashion of the day, from the present King and Queen (then Prince and Princess of Wales), dressed respectively as the Grand Prior of the Order of St John of Jerusalem and Marguerite de Valois, to the newest Radical Member of Parliament gorgeously attired as the Great Mogul. The Duchess of Devonshire, who looked exceedingly well as Zenobia Queen of Palmyra, and the Duke, as the Emperor Charles V, received, on a raised dais at the end of the ball-room, the endless procession who passed by bowing, curtseying or salaaming, according to the characters they represented.[124]

A number of the guests 'were more becomingly than comfortably attired'. There was present, for example, a 'charming Hebe, with an enormous eagle poised on her shoulder and a gold cup in her hand'. Unfortunately, the poor woman (Lady Westmorland, as we saw earlier) tried to preserve the 'perfect picture' that she made all evening, to her great discomfort. Prince Alfred of Edinburgh, disguised as the Duke of Normandy (complete with casque and chain armour), finally had to lift his visor when 'heat and hunger forced him to sacrifice his martial appearance'.[125]

Some guests chose the Ball to make social statements and semiotic codes were used to great effect. One very wealthy duchess, 'famous for her jewels', chose to attend as Charlotte Corday in a cotton skirt and simple mob cap, while another aristocrat, 'trembling on the verge of bankruptcy', chose to make a splash in a costume 'covered with gems of priceless value'. Sir John Kaye attended in chain-mail as his ancestor Sir Kaye of the *Morte d'Arthur*, and the Duke and Duchess of Somerset were stunningly costumed as their forebears.[126]

There were some inevitable disappointments: one 'well-known baronet' had been assiduously 'perfecting himself for weeks in the role of Napoleon, his face and figure lending themselves to the impersonation'. The poor man was dismayed 'at finding in the vestibule a second victor of Austerlitz, even more lifelike and correct than himself. It was indeed another Waterloo for both of them.'[127]

As is usually the case at fancy-dress balls, there was actually very little dancing, Jennie recalled. Indeed, guests were too busy observing everyone's costumes, or trying to preserve their own assumed parts. This could get out of hand, she wrote, as in the example of two gentlemen who, in arguing over the favours of the same young lady, began to fight a duel in the garden. It was an unfair battle, as one combatant was a crusader with a double-handed sword, and his opponent a Louis XV courtier armed solely with a rapier. The courtier got the worst of it, receiving 'a nasty cut on his pale pink silk stocking'.[128]

Again, as is often the case, perhaps the most fun to be had was in reliving the event. Jennie, as a close friend of the Devonshires, was delighted to be invited to Kimbolton, the home of Consuelo, the Duchess of Manchester, the following Saturday, 'where most of the company were persuaded to don their fancy dress once more, and of course the ball was discussed *ad nauseam*. Many were the divergent opinions as to who looked the best, the majority giving the palm to Lady Westmorland.'[129]

Mrs Arthur Paget as Cleopatra

The Marlborough family was one of the most prestigious in the land, but it was not without controversy. Lord Randolph Churchill was a difficult man, and an unreliable political partner, as we have seen. From Jennie's perspective, his early death was, sadly, not just a release but a relief. And his brother Blandford was a social disaster, whose shortcomings affected the whole family and many relations. Florence Williams, a close friend of Bertie's and a firm favourite in social circles, described some of the repercussions of his poor behaviour.

She herself had had to cancel her appearance at the Ball, despite having played a pivotal role in the preparations, as leader of the Italian quadrille. The disappointment was naturally exacerbated because of the weeks of rehearsals and planning the perfect costume, for what she called 'the greatest fancy-dress ball' that she had ever seen. She was especially chagrined because the disappointment was due to the death of her husband's sister Edith, Lady Aylesford, in Paris, and Lady Aylesford had lived in disgrace, estranged from her family. The sad story provides a fascinating example of what happened when boundaries of decorum were breached and social ostracism resulted. While married to the Earl of Aylesford ('Sporting Joe') – a champion polo player and intimate of the Prince of Wales – Edith had embarked on a disastrous and, alas, very public affair with the very unsatisfactory and married George Spencer-Churchill, Lord Blandford (later 8th Duke of Marlborough). In February 1876, Lady Aylesford wrote to her husband, who was on a hunting trip in India with the heir to the throne, telling him that she planned to elope with Blandford. Such unthinkable, scandalous behaviour would hurt not only the families involved (Blandford was married with children), but cast an unwelcome shadow on the Prince himself, and on his social intimates – the nucleus of which was Jennie Churchill, her old school chum Consuelo Mandeville (later Manchester), and Lord and Lady Beresford.[130]

The Earl returned to London at speed, where the two families took legal counsel. Florence's husband Hwfa wanted to challenge Blandford to a duel, and Jennie Churchill's husband Randolph tried to convince his brother to drop the elopement plans. To make the tricky situation infinitely worse, however, Randolph took it upon himself to approach Bertie's wife, telling her that if Bertie's chum Aylesford (whom the Prince supported wholeheartedly) proceeded with the divorce, he would produce the Prince's intimate letters to Lady Aylesford as evidence in court. He informed her that should this occur, it was unlikely that the Prince would ever accede to the throne. The attempted blackmail was an unmitigated catastrophe. Prime Minister Disraeli was told, and the Queen was livid with Randolph. She and Bertie demanded that he make an apology to Alexandra, who should not have been involved in such a sordid mess.

Blandford disappeared to Holland, where his brother joined him. The Marlboroughs were *personae non gratae* in royal circles for years. Inch by inch, other family members crept back into the royal fold. Much to her delight, Florence had been asked to play a major part at the Ball. Now, though, despite Lady Aylesford's disgrace, there was no question of not going into mourning. This is an excellent demonstration of the aristocracy's facility to observe social convention whilst accepting the rigours of royal approval and social Siberia. Despite having shunned the unfortunate Edith for over two decades, the family had to observe the formalities of formal mourning. Florence made arrangements to be replaced at the Ball, though her disappointment was acute: 'London was at its fullest, and there was a spirit of festivity in the air.'

All of her friends were included 'and neither expense nor ingenuity was spared in devising and carrying out the most beautiful costumes'. Numbers of old books – and pictures – had been 'consulted to make sure that the historical figures were accurate in every detail, and in many cases those taking part assumed the characters of famous ancestors'.[131] Mrs Williams had organised the Italian quadrille, and it was quite the prestigious affair. Two Lords Chamberlain – Lords Lathom and Peel – were cast as Doges of Venice and the exquisite Helen D'Abernon and Alice Montagu – one of Consuelo's twins – were in the quadrille. Also part of the ensemble were Lords Alexander Thynne and Wimborne. It was a gay affair: rehearsals were held twice a week and, Florence mused, as in so many instances, the rehearsals were 'often the best part'.

Such was the consternation at the untimely death of Lady Aylesford that the Duchess of Devonshire came round 'at once' to discuss this alarming event. As Florence noted, she had 'been taking such an interest in the arrangements of the quadrille that it was perfectly impossible to drop it, though, of course, it was equally out of the question that I should go to the ball myself'. Lady Plymouth was prevailed upon, and did her part splendidly, while poor Florence dined with her quadrille partners and then spent the night of the party at the top of a staircase viewing through a skylight the brilliant scenes below:

> Never shall I forget the heat we endured as we stood at our observation post. We stayed there till nearly four o'clock in the morning, abandoning it only for a few moments to creep down the back staircase to get something to eat. How I longed to be down in the room! I had thought of nothing else for so long that it was most disappointing....[132]

In spite of the sadness, Florence revelled in the spectacle before her and her companion, Frank Mildmay (later Lord Mildmay), who was also in mourning. 'Tottie' Mezies (later Lady Holford) was quite 'the loveliest in the room', her Titania costume extremely becoming, with its white draperies and an 'enormous bunch of lilies', which 'set off to its full advantage her beautiful long golden hair'. Jennie Churchill's younger sister Leonie Leslie was a 'perfect Brünnhilde', while Harry Stonor (*see page 111*), the senior courtier, made a 'most perfect Lohengrin'.[133] Many guests believed that Sybil, Countess of Westmorland, was a stand-out as 'a perfectly beautiful Hebe'.[134]

As can be seen, the overlap between politician and socialite was significant: Lord Rosebery appeared as an eighteenth-century gentleman while Major John Seymour Wynne Finch, previously aide-de-camp to the Lord Lieutenant of Ireland and member of Special Embassies to Foreign Courts, was a Tuscan duke. The Liberal politician, statesman and writer the Earl of Crewe (Lord Lieutenant of Ireland 1892–95) was resplendent as Philip of Spain.

It was at the Ball that Jennie, widowed after Randolph's tragic early death in 1895 (possibly from syphilis), famously met the handsome George Cornwallis-West, a young British officer some twenty years her junior. He had reluctantly accompanied his sister, Princess Daisy of Pless, a society beauty married to Prince Hans Heinrich XV of Germany. Daisy had led her court as the Queen of Sheba and insisted that George form part of her retinue. The Cornwallis-West family was one of lineage and little money, renowned for truly exceptional beauty. George's mother, known as Patsy, was an Irish-born aristocrat, and had apparently, at the age of sixteen, had an affair with the Prince of Wales. When the affair was discovered she was hurriedly married to William Cornwallis-West, who was more than twice her age. The arrival of three children within the first years of marriage did nothing to dispel persistent rumours that George was Bertie's son.

There was not enough money to maintain the family estates, and George, the only son and a notable *parti*, had been expected to marry a wealthy woman. The Cornwallis-West family were so appalled by George's marriage to Jennie in 1900 that they refused to attend the simple ceremony, and made their disappointment plain. Randolph's widow had two sons of George's age, and insufficient income to support her cash-strapped young husband. When Jennie became engaged, her friends rallied round, and 'among her wedding presents was a diamond and pearl tiara from the Duke and Duchess of Devonshire, A.J. Balfour and other friends'. This was so that she would have a tiara on her wedding day: that of the Cornwallis-West family, traditionally presented to the heir's bride, was retained by his parents.[135]

Consuelo Vanderbilt Marlborough

An American heiress of epic wealth, young Consuelo Vanderbilt had married the Duke of Marlborough in 1895, in a blaze of publicity. Her mother Alva had made no secret of her ambitions to find her only daughter a duke, and she did so with the help of her close American society friends in London: Jennie Churchill, Minnie Stevens (Lady Paget) and Consuelo, Duchess of Manchester, who was young Consuelo's godmother. Lady Paget reputedly was happy to 'bring girls out', for a fee, but whether or not money changed hands, the seventeen-year-old Consuelo, self-admittedly shy and diffident, was placed at a dinner party at the Paget home next to 'Sunny'[136] Marlborough. This was the beginning of a rather lacklustre courtship, and Consuelo described in her memoir how her strong-willed mother eventually had forced her to accept the Duke's proposal. It was for both parties a marriage of convenience. The Marlborough seat at Blenheim was in dire need of investment, and the heir was expected to marry well and start a family. Consuelo had been in love with an American suitor, whom her mother deemed unacceptable. She was ambitious for her daughter, and Consuelo wrote of how she had been forced into the union very much against her will.

There was a softening of her position towards her mother later in life, however, despite the unhappiness of the marriage. Alva, who became a leading women's rights activist, was desperately keen for her daughter to have as broad and impactful a platform as possible. She believed that having the kind of social position offered by the Marlborough connection, leveraged with Vanderbilt millions, could offer Consuelo the kind of social, cultural and political heights to which she herself aspired. But Consuelo, a new bride at eighteen, was more preoccupied with finding her feet as the chatelaine of an immense estate, and as the youngest and one of the most senior of her new rank. She is credited with inventing the phrase 'an heir and a spare' after giving birth to two boys in rapid succession.

The Marlborough couple spent much of their twenty-five-year marriage apart, and both were unhappy with one another, formally separating after eleven years. There had been an inauspicious beginning to the union, when after their honeymoon the young bride had been presented to her husband's grandmother, the formidable Dowager Duchess, a daughter of the 4th Marquess of Londonderry. After a stern lecture on the many duties and responsibilities that lay ahead for her, the Dowager Duchess told Consuelo that her first duty 'was to have a child and it must be a son, because it would be intolerable to have that little upstart Winston become Duke. Are you in the family way?'[137]

The Hon. G. Stanley as Maro (period of Louis XVI)

After the birth of two sons (and there has been speculation on the paternity of her second, Ivor), Consuelo had a number of affairs. She confessed to her husband, who informed her that he had married her for her money to save Blenheim. Jennie's son Winston, Marlborough's cousin, was fond of Consuelo, who brought in many reforms on the estate to help the tenants. She also fought for women's rights, founding the Women's Municipal Party, to help ensure that women were fairly represented in local government. Winston, despite his youth, was a sage counsellor, and provided wise counsel during her marriage woes, helping her to obtain the separation she wanted.

Her photograph from the Ball, taken by the noted photographer Alexander Bassano, was clearly taken after the birth of her first son, known as Blandford, which took place two months after the party. She and her husband attended dressed as French aristocrats, both with elaborate costumes, bedecked by jewels. It would have been a searingly hot, crowded event to attend when seven months pregnant and she recounted walking home through Green Park to Spencer House (a matter of minutes). It was in the early hours, and on the grass she picked her way through the 'dregs of humanity', who were 'too dispirited or sunk to find work or favour, pitiful representatives of the submerged tenth'. She imagined that they must resent her for seeming such 'a vision of wealth and youth', but in fact wrote that they had only looked at her – and 'some even had a compliment to enliven my progress'.[138] It should be observed that much of Consuelo's memoir portrays her, unsurprisingly, in a favourable light,[139] but it is astonishing to imagine the inviolability she felt – even if, no doubt, accompanied – in walking in her finery across the park in the dark. And her comments and descriptions about 'the dregs' were all too prevalent in her privileged milieu.

It took Consuelo some time to achieve her freedom, but she managed it, ultimately marrying the wealthy French aviator that she loved after her divorce was finalised in 1921. She remained politically active, notably with philanthropic activity that benefited women and children. After the Second World War, she retired to the United States, where her life soon became more that of a rich socialite, with magnificent properties in Florida, the south of France and New York. She became reconciled with her formidable mother, who obligingly provided testimony of the forced nature of her marriage to Marlborough, enabling Consuelo and the Duke to obtain an annulment eventually, in 1926.

Daisy 'Babbling' Brooke (Frances, Countess of Warwick)

Daisy Brooke – known as 'Babbling' because of her constant indiscretions, in both letters and conversations – took pride of place as Marie Antoinette, her costume perhaps a clever nod to her status as Bertie's acknowledged mistress-in-chief. The liaison between the renowned beauty and the Prince had led to yet another scandal surrounding the heir to the throne, and hardened negative views about Bertie held by senior figures such as Lord Salisbury, who notoriously refused to host him at his home, Hatfield. In her memoir, Daisy mused on changes in society that had occurred in the late nineteenth century; in particular she was struck by the difference in social and political entertaining. In the past, she mused, every invitation had been 'personal' – indeed, no strangers were solicited or tolerated.

Socialite and huntswoman Lady Augusta Fane concurred, writing that 'society' as it had been understood earlier in the nineteenth century was 'much smaller and more select' than it became in the later part of the century. Hosts took their responsibilities very seriously, she mused, and 'it would have been an unheard-of barbarism to invite people to your house whom you did not know'. Indeed, the host and hostess were 'not merely the caterers of food and music to hordes of strangers'.[140] These parties were the pleasures of the powerful set – beautiful old houses full of 'treasures and wonderful historical memories' were opened to the sounds of music and the scent of flowers. Fane recalled a dance at which the Irish hostess 'had turned her ballroom into a bower of scarlet roses'.[141]

One might assume that this edict restricted numbers, but Daisy wrote of how 'five hundred was no large figure for a political reception, which would start at nine o'clock in the evening and be over at midnight'. These occasions were the height of indulgence and luxury, and the supper would be a buffet, 'of irreproachable quality', for there were 'no sterner critics of champagne, foie gras, quail, and the rest of the familiar luxuries, than the people who attended receptions'.[142] Another huge cost was the 'outlay on floral decorations'. Such was the rage for this that hostesses competed to fill the large rooms with great masses of flowers, which had to be expensively procured from florists if the host did not have access to vast quantities of hothouse flora.

The Duchess of Devonshire, with her five splendid residences, did of course have access to large quantities of greenery and flowers. She ordered train cars to be filled with the very best of the hothouse flowers and plants from the massive family seat at Chatsworth, in Derbyshire. The head gardener accompanied his precious cargo, and a team of gardeners (also from Chatsworth) and arrangers spent the day of the party preparing the rooms and gardens at Devonshire House. The flowers were hung in festoons, arranged in 'huge vases' and in 'banks against the walls'.[143]

Daisy's keen eye made her comments about life at the very top of the social pyramid quite fascinating, and her affair with the Prince guaranteed her access to most functions. She observed that it was 'a costly business' to give the political parties needed to bring together the elite, and she noted that newcomers were making their way into the aristocratic bastions of high society. As we have seen, outsiders – plutocrats, Americans, foreigners – charged into the hallowed halls of social privilege through the auspices of the Prince of Wales and his friends and lovers, and were gradually breaking down traditional barriers to entry.

Daisy is also a fascinating figure because her life was so full of drama. Born in wealth and great social position to Colonel Charles Maynard and his second wife, Blanche FitzRoy, she inherited the family estates on her father's death in 1865, as well as the great family home. Such was her eligibility that she was considered a possible spouse for Queen Victoria's son Prince Leopold (later Duke of Albany). The Queen desired the match, but in the end Daisy – known for her exceptional beauty – married Francis Greville, Lord Brooke, son and heir of the 4th Earl of Warwick. After the birth of her first child, Leopold, Daisy became involved in a number of affairs with high-society men. Lord Charles Beresford was the father of her subsequent two children.

Two more children were born, fathered by her subsequent lover, the millionaire sportsman Joe Laycock. The Prince of Wales was one of Daisy's most devoted lovers, and their affair lasted a decade, following which they remained good friends. Daisy was plagued by scandal, however. Furious at the news that Beresford's wife Mina was pregnant, she apparently wrote an angry letter which was opened in his absence by his spouse, who ultimately gave it to a well-known society lawyer for safekeeping. It then appears that Daisy, in despair, appealed to the Prince of Wales, who himself approached Beresford. It did not go well. Worse, the news got out – Daisy earned her soubriquet 'Babbling Brooke' – and even featured in the press: 'It is said that the breach between Lord Charles Beresford and the Prince of Wales will never now be healed,' ran the story on Christmas Day. Encouraging speculation, the snippet continued by claiming that 'Curious stories are afloat as to the nature of the final quarrel, but probably none are reliable.'[144] And there was more. After hosting a magnificent ball at her home, Easton Hall, in 1895, Daisy was vehemently criticised by the socialist editor of the left-wing *Clarion* newspaper. By her own account, when she went to remonstrate, he converted her to the socialist cause. She subsequently threw herself into supporting social reform and patronising many philanthropic ventures. Sadly, this generosity, and a continued habit of overspending, led to several brushes with bankruptcy – and further scandal, as she threatened to sell the love letters the Prince had sent her to pay off her debts (this was averted by a generous admirer but caused a huge scandal). She published a number of books – two memoirs written primarily to raise money, but also several more serious works on proposed social reforms. There is no doubting Daisy's devotion to her left-wing principles, although they proved no impediment to her enthusiastic attendance at the Ball.

Consuelo Manchester

Yet another of Bertie's closest women friends was Louise's daughter-in-law, Consuelo Yznaga. This friendship reinforces our understanding that there was no uniformity in the group of Americans who left their homes and made their lives in Britain or the continent. These women (for they were predominantly women) were not all from wealthy families, although it was the case for most. Indeed, the only way to meet eligible aristocrats was either to travel abroad, which was expensive, or to encounter potential suitors in a suitable, i.e. elite, environment. American women came from New York, Boston, Philadelphia, Chicago and San Francisco and were of differing backgrounds and education. Consuelo, undoubtedly, was a novelty on both sides of the Atlantic.

Her father, Antonio Yznaga del Valle, was descended from an old Castilian family that had emigrated to Cuba, where they became extremely wealthy sugar planters. He also accumulated estates in Puerto Rico and Cuba.[145] After marrying Ellen Clement, of a distinguished New England family, the young family lived at Ravenswood Place, a plantation in Louisiana that she had inherited. Consuelo and her two sisters spent time in Paris and New York when they were older, and the eldest, their brother Fernando, became a noted stockbroker and man about town. It was at a Paris convent to which Consuelo had been sent to be 'finished' that she met and began a lifelong friendship with Jennie Jerome (later Churchill).

In 1876, after a stay in fashionable Saratoga Springs in upstate New York, Consuelo nursed a feverish Lord Mandeville, heir to the dukedom of Manchester, who was there for the season – openly seeking a rich wife – and she soon became his bride. Their wedding at Grace Church in New York was a massive social event, and it was not long before Consuelo took her place as a beautiful, musical and gracious socialite in London. The Prince of Wales delighted in her banjo playing; it was reputed that she could reproduce any music by ear and she combined this love of music with high spirits and enjoyment.

Her delight in music, her beauty and southern charm made her a great favourite of the Prince and she was soon firmly ensconced in the bosom of the Marlborough House set, bringing in her wake her sisters Natica and Emily. The Duke of Portland recorded admiringly that she 'took Society completely by storm by her beauty, wit and vivacity and it was soon at her

The Hon. Harry Stonor as Lohengrin

very pretty feet'.[146] In spite of her great social success, the young couple were soon faced with a problem common to the Manchester family. Consuelo had grown up wealthy with no sense of budgeting, and the Manchesters as a family had a well-deserved reputation of going through money at an alarming rate. Montagu was no exception, and he and Consuelo were sent to spend long periods in financial exile at the impoverished family estate in Ireland. Like Minnie Paget, Consuelo discovered that there was a lucrative market in marriage brokerage between socially aspirant Americans and members of the British aristocracy attracted by large dowries, and she became adept at performing introductions for a consideration. The rapid disappearance of her large dowry added to the urgency of finding sources of income.

By 1889, the year he succeeded to the title, Mandeville filed for bankruptcy with debts of over £100,000. He was the despair of his mother, Louise, who took comfort in her four other children. By 1890, when he succeeded to the title, Manchester was a notorious inebriate and womaniser, conducting, scandalously, an affair with Bessie Bellwood, a music-hall singer. He and Consuelo lived apart after the births of their son William in 1877 and twin girls, Alice (known as Nell) and Jacqueline (known as May), in 1879. Manchester died, aged only thirty-nine, of cirrhosis of the liver in 1892. It was a squalid end to a squalid life.

With her husband a sad replica of his dissolute father, Consuelo was both pitied and applauded for her courage in putting a brave face to her woes. She was aided in this by her affair with Bertie from the 1880s, filling a gap of serious mistresses between the beautiful actress Lillie Langtry and Daisy Brooke. Like many of the Prince's lovers, they remained good friends once the liaison ended. Her friendship with Bertie, and her close family and love for her daughters, sustained her through the vicissitudes of Manchester's frequent desertions. The two girls were charming and cherished.

Their brother 'Kim' described the first time that the twins met the Queen. Having been extensively briefed by the Princess of Wales on the importance of good behaviour, the toddlers ignored all strictures and immediately climbed on to Her Majesty's lap. This offence was overlooked.

Later, when the monarch picked up her chicken bone for a nibble, the girls 'unable to restrain their horror at witnessing what was, to them, an utter departure from all recognised codes of nursery behaviour, with one accord pointed a finger at Her Majesty, Queen Victoria, Empress of India, and shrieked "Oh, piggy-wiggy!"'[147] Happily, on this occasion, the notoriously dour monarch *was* amused.

The connections to the highest social circles were further reinforced in 1893 when Natica Yznaga married Sir John Lister-Kaye, a Lieutenant in the Horse Guards and senior courtier; Natica and Emily, like the trio of Jerome sisters, remained close all their lives, providing mutual support and love. Their brother Fernando crossed the ocean regularly and became as much of a fixture in London's elite social circles as in those of New York, especially after his marriage to Alva Vanderbilt's sister Jennie Smith. Consuelo inherited the Louisiana plantation as well as other assets on the death of her mother, and retained both her dignity and her place in society. Tragically, both of her cherished daughters died young, aged fifteen and twenty, which was a terrible blow. Her son William also caused her much heartache, as he followed in his father's footsteps and constantly ran out of money.[148] For someone who suffered great hardships, Consuelo was a cheerful companion to the Prince and she was also a great friend to his wife Alexandra.

Despite his great affection for her, Consuelo was not immune to the Prince's ire at any perceived disrespect. They fell out on a number of occasions, but such was the force of her personality that she weathered such storms. She was a woman of spirit and independence. In 1903 she commissioned her own tiara, as the Manchester jewels were long gone. Cartier's records show that she herself supplied over a thousand brilliant-cut diamonds as well as more than 400 rose-cut diamonds. The resulting tiara was magnificent, made of 'graduated flaming hearts and C scrolls inspired by a vision of France before the revolution'.[149] The 'C' was, magnificently, for 'Consuelo'.

JEWISH PATRONAGE: ROTHSCHILDS AND SASSOONS

WE HAVE SEEN THAT THE PRINCE OF WALES – like his mother – was open-minded about outsiders, but this tolerance existed only to a point. Again like the Queen, his acceptance of outsiders had much to do with how useful they were. Improprieties and deviations from royal obeisance were punished in a permanent and draconian fashion. One of the reasons for the Prince's fondness for Hartington was the Duke's strict adherence to royal protocol, despite his easy-going personality. One courtier, in a wry response to a comment on Bertie's 'informality', said: 'Yes, His Royal Highness is always ready to forget his rank, as long as everyone else remembers it.'[150]

In the case of Bertie's Jewish friends, the observance of hierarchy never faltered, and in return he opened previously closed doors to them. He loved to stay at their magnificent London and country houses, bringing his extensive retinue with him. He was clear about his desire to have his friends included at parties, if the hosts wished him to appear. The origin of the warm relations between the Prince and his Jewish friends may have begun in their willingness to finance his overdraft and help with his spending problem by subsidising it, but once these relationships were established, there was more than a financial and social trade at play. The Prince *liked* his Jewish friends; he appreciated their warmth, taste, generosity and love of the arts. Their strong family values echoed his own. When he visited them, every effort was made to accommodate his love of luxury and comfort. Delicious food, splendid entertainment and beautiful surroundings enhanced the Prince's delight in his friends.

Jews had been expelled from Britain in 1290, and it was not until the seventeenth century that resettlement started taking place. Overall numbers remained low; immigration from Eastern Europe grew significantly following the horrors of the pogroms in the Russian Empire during 1881–84, following the assassination of Tsar Alexander II. The British population of 60,000 Jews in 1880 leapt to 300,000 by 1914.[151] The process of integration was one of challenge, as large numbers of poorly educated and usually financially deprived families arrived *in extremis* from Poland

and Russia. The well-established Anglo-Jewish population was faced with the daunting prospect of providing for, and helping, a foreign group into the social, cultural and political life of the nation. Political action was a necessity for the wider community.

It was not until 1858, with the passage of the Jews Relief Act, that Jews were even allowed to take a seat in Parliament, with a modified oath. Of course there had been a convert: Benjamin Disraeli ('Dizzy'), 1st Earl of Beaconsfield, as Conservative Prime Minister, served twice, in 1868 and 1874–80. He was, notoriously, a great flatterer of Her Majesty, and the Queen loved him. Not only had Disraeli converted to Anglicanism at the age of twelve, he had later married a wealthy Anglican widow (marrying outside the faith consolidated his non-Jewish status). Sir Lionel Rothschild served as the first MP, although David Salomons and others had taken part in municipal and other political roles.[152] Still, the Act of 1858 was a major recognition of the importance of the previously unrepresented Jewish population, and the beginning of the integration of the talent and resource of the Jews in Britain. The trend was reinforced when Lord Rosebery married the heiress Hannah Rothschild in 1876.

Concomitantly, as the doors opened to the highest social circles, through the auspices of the Prince the Rothschilds, Sassoons, Bischoffsheims, millionaires such as Sir Ernest Cassel, Baron Hirsch, Alfred Beit and Ludwig Neumann were increasingly included in invitations that revolved around Bertie. Cassel and Hirsch were especially helpful in managing the Prince's financial shortfalls. In time, the integration evolved into an elite form of Anglo-Jewry, and friendships were struck up on their own merits. Many members of the Prince's intimate circle (including the Duchess of Devonshire), the Marlborough House set, turned to the clever bankers for investment advice. Cassel was particularly helpful in this regard. These Anglo-Jewish wealthy families were notoriously generous and free-spending, lavishing luxuries on their social circles. They could be relied upon to subsidise expensive entertainments. The presence of Lady Rothschild, Mrs Leopold Rothschild and Mrs Alfred Sassoon (*see page 151*), on the committee that commissioned the fifty copies of the picture album from the Ball as a gift for their hostess, strongly suggests that they paid for the costly, privately printed book.

As Beatrice Webb, the sociologist and economist who acted as hostess for her father, the international railway magnate Richard Potter, in the 1880s, acidly recorded:

> Like the British Empire, London Society had made itself what it was in a fit of absentmindedness. To foreign observers it appeared all-embracing in its easy-going tolerance and superficial good nature.... But deep down in the unconscious herd instinct of the British governing class there *was* a test of fitness for membership of this most gigantic of social clubs, but a test which was seldom recognized by those who applied it, still less to those to whom it was applied, *the possession of some form of power over people.* The most obvious form of power, and the most easily measurable, was the power of wealth.[153]

And this was indeed the case. We can observe how the broadening of the aristocratic mind came about largely through the pervasive influence of the Prince of Wales: he welcomed his personal financier Sir Ernest Cassel (whose granddaughter was to marry the impeccably connected Lord Louis Mountbatten) and his great friends of the Rothschild family. At his court such men were sought after, and 'in such an atmosphere the adulation of gold and diamond millionaires, financiers, and rough self-made men, became fashionable and respectable'.[154] As these wealthy men and women became more integrated, even the most exclusive and close-minded of the social and cultural elite became more open – with some exceptions and some mixed feeling – to outside influence.

The undisputed leaders of the social set were present at the Jubilee Ball: as well as Balfour, Curzon, Lyttleton and Wyndham there were Lady Elcho, Margot Asquith (*née* Tennant), her sister, the society beauty Lady Ribblesdale, figures such as Millicent, Duchess of Sutherland, and Lady Wimborne. The Tennant sisters – Margot, Laura Lyttleton and Charlotte

Miss Muriel Wilson as Queen Vashti

Ribblesdale – were very much from new money, daughters of an incredibly successful Glasgow industrialist, yet they dominated a certain set, and traditionally had had the power to set the tone. As the Prince of Wales welcomed other plutocrats such as the Wilson and Guinness families, along with his Jewish friends, there were a number of factors that led to a tone less 'exclusive and more tolerant towards the brash display of wealth. One should not discount a broadening of the mind of the old nobility, a greater readiness to accept the non-aristocratic as equals, a liberalization which proceeded quite independently of calculations of personal advantage.'[155]

As the journalist Escott observed, the exclusiveness that had characterised the highest echelons of society had, by the 1890s, gradually eroded. He wrote that the nineteenth century had become 'the Age of Money' – and not merely thousands, but great wealth. 'Disguise it as we may,' he wrote acerbically, 'wealth is the governing force in our social system.'[156] Certainly, money – and the need for it – was far more frequently discussed. In his memoir, the Duke of Somerset was happy to report wryly that Baron Charles Rothschild 'going to pay his usual compliments to the Pope, was significantly informed that His Holiness was not in want of a loan'.[157]

The Jewish community brought the critical element of globalisation of capital, and this led to an opening of the traditional aristocratic mindset, which had hitherto been for the most part limited to 'The Grand Tour' of the ancient and continental capitals and trips to enjoy taking a cure, or gambling in Nice. But when members of the aristocracy, some of whom were already featured prominently on the boards of railway companies, began in the 1890s to take more of an interest in business, 'there was a veritable rush to secure endorsements from aristocrats by encouraging them to sit on boards and by 1896 there were 167 noblemen, over a quarter of the peerage, holding directorships, most of them in more than one company'.[158] Financial networks extended well beyond Britain and her Empire's borders. When investing their funds, friends of Bertie's placed their capital in Russian railways, Australian mines, American industry and others.

The reliance on mainly Jewish financiers strengthened the bonds between British aristocrats and Bertie's friends. Investment in home industrial activity, such as breweries, local collieries and retailers, was accompanied by placements in South African gold mines, Indian and South American railways and other speculations on the advice of men such as Cassel, Wernher and the Rothschild clan. Disproportionately represented among the very wealthiest of England, the huge fortunes were for the most part accumulated via the Stock Exchange. Indeed, British savings were poured into the hands of the City of London traders and bankers – no other nation has ever placed so much of its national income in capital investment abroad.[159]

The Rothschilds

The formidable Rothschild clan led the way: the firm of N.M. Rothschild, established in 1809 by Nathan Mayer Rothschild, was the first to establish itself as a dominant investment house in Britain, with a vast international network with whom to create joint-stock shares and loans. The Rothschild family set up banks in various European capitals, and the era of global capital and international finance began. The Prince, with his wealthy friends, was all too ready to benefit from the huge profits. Rothschild cash was enormous: as early as 1879 the dynasty was believed to control £100,000,000 in capital[160] (£15 billion in today's values).

It seemed as though money could be magicked through the hands of the experts, and Britain's regulations were the most permissive of Europe.[161] The Stock Exchange continued its seemingly unstoppable growth, and a magnificent new building was opened in 1885. The British pound was backed by the gold standard and became the international currency. In this heady atmosphere of easy profits, companies were established overnight, many of them fronted by boards featuring cash-strapped British aristocrats happy to lend their names to businesses of which they understood little. Thus did speculation run rife – as did grumbles of animosity towards the successful Jewish bankers.

The cosmopolitan and international interjection of energy and new ideas that characterised Bertie's alternative court shone far more brightly

than that of the staid and static Victoria. The Prince's entourage also
became far more international. London's 'Age of Ostentation' embraced
the Rothschilds, Baron Hirsch, Ernest Cassel, Alfred Beit and others
from Germany; the Sassoons came from Baghdad by way of Bombay and
Shanghai, and of course there were the fabulously wealthy Americans and
South African diamond magnates. And such fortunes had been made in
international markets. Hirsch's vast wealth had, 'it was rumoured', been
made 'when he built a railroad for the Turkish Government who contracted
to pay the Baron by the mileage, and did not insist on the shortest route!'[162]

From the Prince's Cambridge days, Nathaniel Rothschild and his
brother Alfred subsidised Bertie, whose allowance was insufficient for
his compulsive hunting and gambling. Mayer Amschel Rothschild was
'delighted' to entertain the Prince at the Derby in 1864 and 1866.[163] Bertie
dined regularly with Leo, Alfred, Ferdinand and Natty on both formal and
informal occasions.[164] This socialising, in Britain and also in France, was
accompanied by sustained financial support from various family members.
Records in Nathaniel Rothschild's archive provide evidence of a £100,000
'loan' made in 1889, followed by another 'loan' (there is no record of any
repayment) of £60,000 in 1893.[165] The Queen was horrified to learn of her
son's debt of 'a large sum owing to Sir A. de Rothschild'.[166]

The heir's financial woes – despite an annuity from Parliament of
£39,000 in addition to his income from the Duchy of Cornwall of over
£50,000 – were well known to his entourage, and the refusal of Parliament
to increase his annuity without further scrutiny of his finances led Bertie
to seek help from moneylenders. There were hushed stories of the heir
holed up in a Paris hotel in the 1880s, surrounded by creditors. Discussions
in the House of Commons regarding the value for money provided by
the monarchy were worrying, and fuelled demands by republicans for an
abolition of the institution. When reports of the Prince and his Marlborough
House set's high-spending splurges were published, republican clubs were
strengthened – there were protests thinly disguised as trade union gatherings
and in the House there was opposition to large allowances proposed for
Victoria's children.

Bertie became ever more determined to avoid provoking more questions about his expensive lifestyle. To put this in perspective, the average annual income per head was £42.70 in 1901.[167] His debts were a matter of great concern to his mother and to Parliament, where his finances were, humiliatingly, openly discussed.[168] A radical MP from Glamorgan, Mr Abraham, argued that holding a levee, unveiling a statue, dining at Mansion House and then seeing part of *Figaro* at the opera house hardly constituted 'a hard day's work!'[169] 'Natty' came to the rescue, offering 'loans' for which the Prince was warmly grateful. One of the ways in which the Prince showed his gratitude to the family was by successfully lobbying for Lionel Walter Rothschild to become a trustee in 1899 of the British Museum, a hugely prestigious nomination. The Austrian Baron Maurice Hirsch was another wealthy Jewish friend who was delighted to pay off the Prince's debts in return for a special place in his social circle – he was said to have 'loaned' the profligate royal an astonishing £600,000 in 1890.[170] Hirsch and many members of the Rothschild clan were guests at the Ball.

Not all of Bertie's set were as eager to befriend the Rothschilds, who were proud of their heritage and not intimidated by the British royal family. Their financial abilities were equalled by their appreciation of the arts, and they were undoubtedly the 'royalty' of the Jewish community. Indeed, one intimate of the family remarked that knowing them as she did, she 'could see how strongly like a Royal Family the Rothschilds are in one respect, namely that they all hate one another but are united as against the world'.[171] The phenomenal acumen, networking and success of the family did not go unnoticed. Daisy Warwick recorded drily that the wealthy Jewish plutocrats were 'resented'. Not 'because we disliked them', she explained, 'but because they had brains and understood finance'. As a class, the aristocracy 'did not like brains', and indeed, their only understanding of money 'lay in the spending, not the making of it'.[172] Lord Balcarres (later 27th Earl of Crawford), a 'patrician to his fingertips'[173] and a consummate member of 'The Great and the Good', sitting on and chairing a number of boards of national cultural institutions, recalled his thoughts after attending a party hosted by Alfred Rothschild (*see page 153*) and Lord Rosebery to meet the Prince of Wales:

The number of Jews in this palace was past belief. I have studied the anti-semite question with some attention, always hoping to stem an ignoble movement; but when confronted by the herd of Ickleheimers and Puppenbergs, Raphaels, Sassoons, and the rest of the breed, my emotions gain the better of logic and justice.[174]

And he was not alone; Balcarres observed that after Edward had ascended the throne, there had been some cries of 'King of the Jews' at an Army Review, and that 'there is much dormant anti-semitism', especially directed at royal patronage.[175]

It is important to recognise that it was certainly the case that not all Jews in Britain were wealthy – indeed, it has been argued that the spotlight on the rich Jewish 'court' surrounding Bertie did a grave disservice to the Jewish population living in misery in London's East End and elsewhere.[176] The wealth of some of these socially prominent families was quite extraordinary, however, and marriages consolidated the fortunes.

T.H. Escott, the editor of the *Fortnightly Review*, wrote dismissively in 1885 as 'A Foreign Resident': 'English society once ruled by an aristocracy is now dominated by a plutocracy. And this plutocracy is to a large extent Hebraic in its composition. There is no phenomenon more noticeable in society than the ascendancy of the Jews.' Escott claimed that this development was the result of the financial power so appealing to the Prince of Wales, who 'regards the best class of Jews with conspicuous favour'.[177] Such concerns were not only enunciated by the cream of society; there were also worries throughout the social groups about the increasing number of immigrants.

In a foreshadowing of now familiar tropes, there were those who claimed that Jewish and other immigrants lived cheaply, and undercut local wages. The repeal of wartime legislation in 1826 had opened the ports of Britain to immigrants with no restrictions, and sixty years later a first public meeting to call for a new measure of statutory restriction was held in the East End. The immigration question was thenceforth 'driven by a mixture of apprehension and fear among the propertied classes in the face of the outcast masses'. There was also opposition from a host of trade unionists

Mr Leopold de Rothschild as Duc de Sully

who were unhappy at the failures of new immigrants to unionise.[178]

There was thus concern over a perceived over-supply of cheap labour and poor living conditions. There was also a general consensus on all sides 'that whenever English workmen and Jewish immigrants came into competition the Jewish workman had the advantage over the Englishman on account of his "lower standard of comfort"'.[179] Amid concerns about uncontrolled immigration, Lord Salisbury introduced an Aliens Bill into the House of Lords in 1894, explaining that there was a danger that Britain's well-known hospitality could be abused by anarchists plotting terror across Europe. He was also exercised by the habits of foreigners undercutting local labour, because 'possessed of a lower standard of life, they dragged down the price of unskilled labour and added to the burden of the ratepayers'. Indeed, there had been in 1892 'a scare that the unusually large migration of Jews from the Russian Empire which had taken place in the previous two years would be repeated'. By the end of the nineteenth century, concerns about immigration – invading the housing market, for example – 'once again acquired great urgency' and once again 'there was a similar breadth of agreement'.[180]

The Rothschilds, Sassoons, Alfred Beit and Sir Ernest Cassel (all present at the Ball) might make money for their aristocratic clients, they might sponsor the arts and entertain lavishly at the racecourse and in their London and country homes, but the immigration question and deep-seated anti-Semitic feelings held by some led to a willingness to accept and delight in lavish hospitality, whilst at the same time mocking the vulgarity and comfort that had been enjoyed. The unpleasant remarks might have reflected the threat that some believed these Jewish families presented. Minnie Paget, an American heiress married to a British aristocrat, observed drily that the Prince shared 'the same taste as the Semites, the same love of pleasure and comfort'.[181]

Nevertheless, socialites delighted in spending their weekends in luxurious country houses. The Rothschilds entertained with splendour in their homes at Gunnersbury, Newmarket and at Ascott, Wing. The furnishings were stupendous, and the gardens exquisite. Florence Williams wrote of 'the lovely long rooms' at Ascott, from which one saw 'a vista of the most perfect garden imaginable, winding down a stretch of open country' which had been designed by Leo Rothschild (*see page 123*) himself. The spring season was especially magnificent, with 'the cherry trees and beds of flowering shrubs and tulips, forget-me-nots and irises' making 'the most perfect setting'.[182]

Hartington and Louise as Duchess of Manchester had enjoyed a friendship with the Rothschilds as early as the 1870s. Disraeli wrote of a dinner party he had attended hosted by Baron Lionel de Rothschild where he met Louise – 'delightful though a little noisy, too shrieking in her merriment' and 'Harty-Tarty'.[183] Baron Nathaniel Rothschild, between 1874 and 1885, built the magnificent Waddesdon Manor in Buckingham to display his stupendous arts collection, and to entertain his friends. The Prince was a frequent guest, and the Manor also served as a political base, where political figures could meet with discretion in the height of comfort and luxury. The Rothschilds actively supported a Tory Unionist alliance in opposition to Gladstone's proposed Home Rule legislation and Arthur Balfour wrote to his uncle Lord Salisbury on 15 June 1886 that he had attended a 'coalition party' at Waddesdon, including 'Chamberlain, Hartington & his Duchess, Randolph, H. Chaplin, etc'.[184]

The Rothschild influence was more than political. Hospitality was an important function of life, and the Rothschild family members – Natty, Alfred, Leopold and others – were generous party-givers. Fancy-dress balls were a feature of this hospitality; the Rothschilds and other wealthy Jewish families often hosted such parties, and many had guests photographed for a family album.[185] In fact, there is every chance that Louise was inspired by Rothschild fancy-dress parties and at the Jewish holiday of Purim, fancy-dress balls celebrated by the Jewish communities in New York and other cities were avidly reported by the press.

In the 1860s, arrangements were made, with a 'blaze of light and color', to transform New York's

staid Academy of Music into a 'Palace of Persepolis,' replete with 'Oriental flourishes' of carpets, 'rainbow-colored' drapery, tassels, cords, and crimson banners, vermilion-colored palm leaves, and gilded columns. Though it harked back to antiquity, the mise-en-scène wasn't without the latest bells and whistles, either. 'Brilliant' jets of gaslight framed the words 'Merry Purim,' which, illuminated, hung in midair, suspended from the ceiling.[186]

Although dressing up in costume was not necessarily part of the Purim celebration, the custom was revived at fundraising balls, especially in New York. The fancy dress was a hugely popular feature:

Equally extravagant, fanciful costumes upped the ante. While some of the female guests came dressed as Queen Esther, far more took their cue from, and channeled, Madame Pompadour. Harlequins, dominoes in all sorts of color combinations, clowns and Columbines were a sight to behold, as was the 'democratic' mix of lords and ladies, Irishmen and 'darkies,' men dressed as women and women garbed in 'outré men's attire'—a symbol, related a reporter named Damocles, of the 'coming woman,' whose advent will one day astonish mankind.[187]

The annual event became so popular that people outside the Jewish community began to attend. The lavish, extraordinary entertainments were so beautiful, the food so spectacular and the arrangements so delightful that a competition for tickets ensued. As was reported:

growing numbers of non-Jews sought to attend an unmistakably Jewish event prompting *Littell's Living Age* in 1868 to observe with barely concealed astonishment that even the 'descendants of the Puritans seek with anxiety tickets to the masked ball of Purim.' The *American Hebrew*, in turn, found the presence of non-Jews heartening. That the 'doors were open wide enough for good Christian society to enter' was sure to put an end to all that 'silly talk' about the 'exclusiveness' of the Jews, the weekly predicted.[188]

Marie, wife of Leopold de Rothschild, attended as Zobeida and was much admired.[189]

The Sassoons

Often referred to as 'the Rothschilds of the east', the Sassoon dynasty claimed to have been descended from King David, and had kept their faith through hundreds of centuries and thought of themselves as leaders in the exiled Jewish community.[190] Unlike the Rothschilds, whose origins lay in Europe, the Sassoons were based in Baghdad; David Sassoon moved further east to Bombay, where in 1832 he founded a new business, a trading company that went on to become one of the most successful in the world, and brought the family immense wealth, including an expansion to Shanghai. Like the Rothschilds, David, who had married twice, deployed his sons – eight in total – throughout Europe, exercising close control and driving the growth of the business.

Trade was the basis of the family's fortunes. As one commentator noted, 'Silver and gold, silks, gums and spices, opium and cotton, wool and wheat – whatever moves over sea or land feels the hand or bears the mark of Sassoon & Co.'[191] David Sassoon, by 1871, gained such control of the opium trade in India that he 'was able to dictate prices at the opium markets in Calcutta' and had taken 'control of the opium markets on both sides of India'.[192] This trade proved extraordinarily lucrative, and the family opened branches along the transit routes for the drug, setting up offices in Singapore, Shanghai and Hong Kong.[193]

In 1858, David Sassoon was sent to London, where he was later joined by his brothers and half-brothers Albert Abdullah, Reuben and Arthur. They were immensely rich, and made no secret of their wealth, acquiring superb properties in London, Surrey, Brighton and Hove. The family members invested heavily in their communities; the magnificent Middle Street synagogue in Brighton bore trademark 'Moorish' touches beloved by the Sassoons.

Although the family were keen to penetrate the sanctums of the highest social ranks, they did not pretend to be other than a prominent Mizrahi Jewish family of eastern origins. Although there were soon marriages into the most select of important Ashkenazi families such as the Rothschilds, the Sassoons were proud to bear the 'Oriental' label associated with them. Happy to play on their 'otherness', the Sassoon brothers soon became fixtures in high society, especially after befriending the Prince of Wales. There was a move away from Arabic custom favoured by David; his London-based sons preferred English tailoring, and Albert Abdullah wished to be addressed as Albert, Abraham as Arthur. Albert named his son Edward in honour of his friend the Prince.

For these huge philanthropists, in India and in Britain, the honours came in both countries. In 1890, a baronetcy was created for Albert. Like the Rothschilds, the Sassoons set their social sights high, but without compromising their allegiance to their faith. Albert's coat of arms, created with the help of the College of Heralds, comprised 'the lion of Judah carrying the rod that was never to depart from their Jewish tribe; a palm tree representing the flourishing of the righteous man; and a pomegranate, a rabbinical symbol of good deeds'.[194] Bertie, who had lobbied for the honour, was initially disappointed at the omission of his friend's name from the list – after he complained, an 'immediate' telegram was sent to reassure the Prince that it had been an oversight, and that Salisbury had approved the nomination.[195] The title was inherited by Albert's son Edward, who had been brought up as a privileged English gentleman, studying at the University of London, shooting with the Prince of Wales and eventually becoming an officer of the Duke of Cambridge's Hussars.

A dynastic merging of two of the wealthiest families in the world took place when, in 1887, Edward married Aline de Rothschild. The ceremony took place in Paris, conducted by the Chief Rabbi of France and attended by 1,200 guests at the Rothschild mansion, on Avenue de Marigny. The couple made a spectacular debut in London society: Edward was a talented sportsman, and Aline had a scholarly knowledge of art and literature. She and Edward – who had political ambitions – created a salon, and their large

The Hon. Mrs Reginald Talbot as a Valkyrie

circle of friends included the authors Sir Arthur Conan Doyle and H.G. Wells as well as artists such as John Singer Sargent. They remained close friends with Bertie, and Aline was one of the few able to inhabit both the Marlborough House set and that of the more rarefied Souls. Their son Philip would go on to achieve a successful political career, and their daughter Sybil would marry into the English aristocracy when she wed George, Earl of Rocksavage, heir of the Marquess of Cholmondeley. (Many of Sybil's Rothschild relations refused to attend the ceremony and cut off contact due to disappointment that she had married 'out'.) After their marriage, Sybil used her enormous artistic talents – and huge fortune – to restore Houghton Hall, home of the nation's first Prime Minister, Horace Walpole.

The Sassoons, through their wealth and great friendship with the Prince of Wales, thus became important figures, with impact, at first without losing their identity. Philip and Sybil, however, of Arab Jewish origins, became far more integrated into the political, cultural and social world of British high society, and we can follow a gradual reduction of 'otherness' that had so characterised their grandparents and, to a lesser extent, their parents (Edward was born in what was then known as Bombay). The Sassoon and Rothschild families' experience in Britain provides compelling examples of how the British elite found ways to accommodate outsiders, especially ones with links to imperial territories. It was not a one-way process. These newcomers were keen to improve general understanding of Jewish history and culture.

With Bertie's endorsement, for example, Reuben Sassoon sponsored a magnificent 'Anglo Jewish Historical Exhibition' in 1887 at the Royal Albert Hall. Both the Rothschild and Sassoon families were hugely generous and public philanthropists.

But anti-Semitism was certainly a prevalent feature of British life, despite Bertie's patronage. Although his Jewish friends were admitted – at the Prince's demand – to the most elite social events, there was systemic and systematic sniping behind the lines. *Sporting Life* sneeringly published the following: 'Sir Albert Abdullah Sassoon, That Indian auriferous coon, Has bought an estate called Queen's Gate, And will enter upon it in June.'[196]

And when Violet Asquith (daughter of Herbert) stayed with Aline and Sybil in 1904 when she was seventeen, she disobligingly referred to Lady Sassoon as 'Sassbags', and wrote of how pleased she would be to escape 'Semite patronage and hot rooms'.[197]

ANCESTRAL VOICES

Sir Algernon West recalled a Christmas dinner hosted by Baron Alfred Rothschild, where 'eight nationalities were represented', namely 'Prince Duleep Singh (*see page 63*), Indian; Baron Alphonse [de Rothschild], French; the Brazilian and Belgian Ministers; Mrs Sassoon, Austrian; Mr ––, a German; M. de Soveral, Portuguese; and ourselves [English]'.[198]

Prince Victor Duleep Singh

The signing of the Treaty of Lahore in 1846 marked the end of the First Anglo-Sikh War, a victory for the British laboriously achieved, thanks to betrayals on the Indian side at critical moments. The fatherless seven-year-old Maharajah Duleep Singh, son of Maharajah Ranjit Singh of Lahore, the 'Lion of the Punjab' and founder of the Sikh Empire, would, apparently, be 'protected' by a British resident and troops, until he turned sixteen. The British would leave as friends – the garrison and expenses paid for by Duleep. Despite the bitter protestations of his mother, in 1849 the young Prince was made to sign a new treaty of surrender, effectively ceding control of the Punjab to the British along with, explicitly, the famous Koh-I-Noor ('Mountain of Light') diamond, the largest in the world. His distraught mother, Rani Jindan, was sent to live in exile. The Koh-I-Noor, worn strapped to the maharajah's bicep, was a potent symbol of power and spirituality for the Sikhs – its value priceless.

The diamond was sent to England, and formally presented to the Queen. It was subsequently re-cut. Duleep's process of Anglicisation, under the care of foster parents, resulted in a conversion to Christianity, and was completed when at the age of fourteen he moved to England, where he was welcomed by the Queen with enormous affection. Victoria was immediately taken with the young Duleep, who was a particularly beautiful young man, and commissioned her favourite court artist, Winterhalter, to paint his portrait. The young man was coaxed into officially presenting the Queen with the diamond, setting to rest any feelings of guilt that she harboured about its forcible acquisition. Duleep found himself in London with nothing to do and plenty to spend. He became a member of the Garrick, the Marlborough, the East India and the Oriental clubs (but was turned down by White's!). At the Alhambra night club, he was seen 'every evening' waving around jewellery to distribute to the artistes.[199]

His escapades did not, however, alienate the Queen. When he later married and had a son, she insisted that the baby, named Albert Victor, born in 1866, be christened at Windsor Castle, and she stood as godmother. The Maharajah continued his dissolute lifestyle while fathering his family, frequenting nightclubs and paying off mistresses. The children were raised in an unhappy household. The boy Victor, as he became known, was educated as an Englishman, attending Eton, then Trinity College, Cambridge, followed by Sandhurst, where he adopted all the behaviours and accoutrements of a spoiled member of the elite, running up huge debts wherever he went. Ponies, women, gambling, drinking swallowed up the large allowance paid to him in exchange for the territories and property that he had given up to the British. Meanwhile his father had become disenchanted by Britain and the British, especially after reuniting with his mother in 1861.

After travelling to see her in India, Duleep had brought his mother, prematurely aged and unwell, to live in Britain. She, filled with bitterness, complained unceasingly about the 'theft' of the Koh-I-Noor, and Duleep soon agreed with her at the injustice, transmitting his views to his son. They began to refer to Victoria as 'Mrs Fagin' in reference to the criminal featured in Charles Dickens's famous novel *Oliver Twist*.[200]

Sadly, Victor followed in the footsteps of his father, whose problems with finances (begging letters to the Queen were a frequent occurrence), drink and women led him to an early grave in 1893. Victor became the ruler of the Royal House of Punjab, and in 1898 resigned his Royal Dragoon Commission, bedevilled by debts. He was a familiar socialite, a close friend of Bertie, and, from childhood, of George Herbert, son of the 4th Earl of Carnarvon and, famously, the financier of Howard Carter's excavation of the Tomb of Tutankhamun. The links and fine web of social connections and historical events were manifested when Lord Carnarvon married Almina Wombwell, believed to be the illegitimate daughter of Alfred Rothschild (who provided an enormous dowry).

Victor Singh's marriage in 1898 was a sensation: the first time an Indian had married a member of the British aristocracy. There was considerable resistance to the match, and it was through the personal intervention of the Prince of Wales that Lady Anne Coventry and Victor Singh were married. Apparently, the Queen supported the alliance, but told Lady Anne never to have children with Victor, and not to live in England. The marriage was childless, and the couple travelled constantly, staying with friends abroad until the welcome wore out.

Victor Singh attended the Ball, dressed, significantly, in Mughal magnificence. As Akbar the Great, his short and stout form is immortalised in a Bassano portrait included in the album presented to the Duchess of Devonshire. The symbolism of his stunning costume, complete with turban and sword and covered in jewels, was potent: Akbar was the greatest Mughal emperor of India, reigning from 1556 to 1605. He was an extraordinarily successful ruler and reformer, creating a centralised financial system and tax collection processes. His central administration system was particularly adept – along with his personal outlook of curiosity and religious tolerance – at securing the loyalty of diverse multi-faith populations.

For Victor Singh, who was to be declared bankrupt – yet again – some five years later, the historical figure he chose to represent could not have been further from his own character. Dissolute, constantly broke, his saving grace was a charm that generated great loyalty from his friends, notably the Prince of Wales. The Earl of Carnarvon often lent the Singhs his home when they stayed in England. But the rancour felt by the Sikh population at the downfall of the proud house of the Lion of Punjab was echoed by that felt by the Prince himself. In 1947, the newly independent government of India officially requested the return of the Koh-I-Noor, which had been re-fashioned into a consort's crown. This was denied, as have been many subsequent requests – which have become more thorny as rulers from Pakistan, Afghanistan and Iran have produced claims for ownership. The present Queen, notably, did not wear the crown at the coronation in order to avoid a diplomatic discourtesy.

Grand Duke Mikhail Mikhailovich Romanov

> Belonging as I do, to the Imperial Blood, and being a member of one of the reigning Houses, I should like to prove to the world how wrong it is in thinking – as the majority of mankind are apt to do – that we are the happiest beings on the earth. There is no doubt that financially we are well situated, but is wealth the only happiness in this world?[201]

The Grand Duke (*see page 69*), known to his family and intimates as 'Miche-Miche', was a proud member of the Romanov dynasty, the third child and second son of seven, the grandson of Tsar Nicholas I of Russia. The Grand Dukes lived as lords: each had huge personal landed estates, with armies of servants. In a country where millions lived in squalor and were illiterate, the Romanovs, who had ruled the nation since 1613, lived a life apart. They were, simply, phenomenally wealthy. In the middle of the nineteenth century, the grand dukes held – and this was government holdings alone – an area greater than four times the size of France. The arable lands were cultivated and managed by serfs and employees and brought them millions in revenue. There were, in addition, huge personal estates and mineral concessions. As one journalist acidly commented in 1905: 'The country is a money-making concern maintained for the benefit of the Romanovs, who give in return a little government, the glory of their

Lord Iveagh as a gentleman at the time of Louis XIII

countenance, and many foul examples of sensuality and extravagance to a king-worshipping people.' Indeed, the grand dukes of the Imperial House of Russia lived on the country 'like a pillaging enemy'.[202]

Apart from military service, nothing was expected of the grand dukes and they lived for the most part dissolute lives of travel to continental capitals, wining and dining and spending vast sums of money. Mikhail proved no exception to the general rule. A tall, handsome man, he loved the military life, 'with endless parties, dancing and gambling'.[203] Yet although he was a royal, the grand duke experienced challenges when seeking to marry. At twenty-five, his efforts were in earnest, and he was first refused by the daughter of Ludwig IV of Hesse, and then by Bertie's daughter Princess Louise. Marrying a commoner was strictly forbidden, but this proved no impediment to a number of further proposals. After Tsar Alexander III banned his putative union with Countess Catherine Ignatiev because she was not royal, Mikhail was sent abroad.

In Biarritz, he met the married Countess Sophie Merenberg, daughter of the Prince of Nassau, whose maternal grandfather was the famous Russian poet Alexander Pushkin. Despite the outright unsuitability of the match, her divorce ensued and the couple were married in 1891. Alexander III banned Mikhail from Russia and the couple made their home in Britain and on the French Riviera, where the Duke's luxurious lifestyle and spending habits earned him the sobriquet 'Uncrowned King of Cannes'. Disowned by his father, the pair turned their backs on Russia, and Sophie was granted the title Countess de Torby (*see page 69*) by her relative the Prince of Waldeck and Pyrmont.

When the new Tsar, Nicholas II, revoked the ban on Mikhail and his wife in 1894, they were reconciled with the family. As one British newspaper observed, however, the pair did not 'take up their life in Russia again, preferring golf at Cannes, hunting and shooting in England and Scotland'.[204] They enjoyed the magnificence of their country estate, Keele Hall in Staffordshire (now part of Keele University campus), and a splendid home in Regent's Park in London.

Mikhail and Sophie were seen as a couple who had given up everything for love. The Grand Duke was stripped of his military titles, and much of his income (although he remained immensely rich). They attended the Jubilee Ball as the French king Henri IV and his beloved mistress, Gabrielle D'Estrées. Known as Henry the Good, or Henry the Great, Henri IV was a hugely successful military commander, and Gabrielle provided him, despite her unofficial status, with counsels and much support, accompanying him – even when pregnant – on the military trail, sleeping in his tent. Henri IV provided France with a lasting legacy of religious conciliation and improved administration. Gabrielle D'Estrées was instrumental in conciliating Catholics and Protestants, until then engaged in a bitter struggle.

In channelling military prowess and successful leadership, Mikhail was nailing his colours to a mast – albeit one far removed from his own country. He had taken such pride in his military career and losing it would not have been easy. But he had married for love. In portraying a couple renowned for their success, and for mutual devotion (Henri had planned to divorce his wife in order to marry his lover), Mikhail and Sophie made a strong statement of their own love story of no regrets, with, perhaps, a longing to be known for something more.

The couple had three children, and their eldest daughter, Anastasia ('Zia'), married, in 1917, Harold Augustus, second son of Sir Julius and Lady Wernher. Julius Wernher was an extraordinary man: born in Germany, he had worked as a clerk before serving as an officer in the Franco-Prussian conflict, where he was present in Paris with the victorious Germans in 1870. After working in a low-level business job in London, Wernher was introduced to the embryonic South African mining industry. After he formed a partnership with Alfred Beit, a Jewish-German businessman of enormous drive, the company went on to dominate the diamond business, and both men became extraordinarily wealthy. Both were philanthropists and great collectors. Beit and Wernher each chose to live in England, where their friendship with the Prince of Wales – and their riches – opened many doors, and they became prominent members of the high-ranking British establishment.

Wernher married Alice Mankiewicz (a socialite and clever musician known as Birdie), of a Polish-Jewish and English background, and they set themselves up, early in the century, at the magnificently remodelled Luton Hoo estate in Bedfordshire. The historic property, lavishly decorated, housed a splendid art collection, and when Harold married Zia, the collection was further enhanced by her own collection of artefacts, including priceless works by Fabergé, the Russian imperial court jeweller.

Financial problems for the Grand Duke and his Countess were already evident in 1916, when he wrote to his cousin, Nicholas II, asking for some help with wedding costs for his daughter Nadejda (Nada), who married the serving naval officer Prince George of Battenberg[205] in November 1916 (the request was unsuccessful). George was a prince of the royal Hessian family and his mother was Princess Victoria, a granddaughter of Queen Victoria. Despite the prestigious ancestry, there was little in the family coffers for the new groom, who had to turn to his mother-in-law for help. Problems continued for the Grand Duke: the Russian Revolution, begun in 1917, decimated his wealth. That year Russian nobles were stripped of their assets, and until his death in 1923 Mikhail and his wife had to retrench their extravagant lifestyles significantly, much to their dismay. Writing in the third person, Grand Duke Mikhail wrote to Balfour in the Foreign Office: 'His Imperial Highness is entirely without means for his living requirements and has no capital or money here.' He then asked for a temporary loan, which was refused, and he and his wife had to leave their sumptuous home in Kenwood and take up residence in a home in Regent's Park in London.[206] An appeal was made to King George V, and he and his wife Mary agreed to lend the couple £10,000. This was, however, insufficient, and it is possible that Zia felt it incumbent upon her to find a wealthy husband. Certainly she would have very little money of her own, and she had been accustomed to a very luxurious style of life. She had known Harold Wernher for many years, and the pair were wed in July 1917. Julius Wernher had died in 1912, and his widow was presented with 'a very large bill after the wedding'. As Zia had no marriage settlement, Birdie settled a large sum on her in the event that Harold – a serving soldier – be killed in action. When Harold reached the age of twenty-six, he gave his parents-in-law 'an undisclosed sum of money on behalf of Zia for some of their important Fabergé collection'.[207]

At the end of the First World War, Harold was still in Italy, where he received letters that were 'not quite begging' from the Duke. Given that Zia's brother (known as Boy) did not have a job, Harold was disinclined to support him, telling his father-in-law that he was not 'going to encourage Boy to do nothing by giving him an allowance now. Of course it must be an awful come-down for them to have absolutely nothing after having had so much but I think it is a pity that they talk about it so openly.'[208] The Wernhers continued to support the Grand Duke, whose distress at the situation in Russia was amplified by the execution of his cousin and family. The King and Queen were also pressed.

The Wernher unions with the Mountbattens and Romanovs provided both families with huge cash injections. The Wernher fortune continued to supply seemingly inexhaustible funds. Harold, eventually the heir after the death of his elder brother, consolidated and grew the fortune. He 'discreetly' helped the Milford Havens with their finances.[209] But the Harold Wernher line has remained enormously rich. A descendant is the 7th Duke of Westminster, who currently holds a fortune estimated at over £9 billion. In another example of the links and integration of great wealth and strong power, Sir Ernest Cassel's daughter Edwina married George's brother, Louis Mountbatten, and they became the last Viceroy and Vicereine of India. Thus another Ball guest – and friend of Bertie – provided much-needed funds to the extended royal family. And the Wernher family have become fully integrated into the fabric of the British aristocracy and royalty.[210]

The Duke and Duchess of Somerset

Magnificently attired as his famous ancestor, 1st Duke and Lord Protector of England during the reign of his nephew Edward VI, the Duke of Somerset made a remarkable figure at the party. The historical links were further reinforced by his wife's appearance as the 1st Duke's sister, Jane Seymour, third wife of Henry VIII and mother of Edward VI. The Duchess was especially successful in her portrayal, an accurate representation of the illustrious portrait by Hans Holbein. The couple looked dashing and impressive, and traced an allusion to the deep and rich history of the nation in Tudor times and the great prominence of the family then.

Examining the antecedents of the title, though, provides a fascinating glimpse at the ingenuity and powers of re-creation of the British aristocracy. The Somerset title has been associated primarily with two families, the Beauforts and the Seymours. The title can be traced back to the twelfth century, a creation of Empress Matilda, but was ultimately not recognised. A series of further creations – and dissolutions – mirrors the political vicissitudes of rule in England that followed. In one example, John Beaufort, son of John of Gaunt, was created Earl of Somerset in 1397; the title was revoked, and premature deaths, changes in regime and other circumstances led to various titles bestowed and then rendered extinct.

Even the family's ascent to royal heights led to what had become a familiar downfall, as the Lord Protector was ultimately executed for treason. The line survived, however. Despite a remarkable number of childless heirs, the genealogy is convincing and demonstrative of a survival instinct in the extant Somerset family. In 1897, the Duke and Duchess were prominent members of the elite, owners of a number of landed estates, including the large property of Maiden Bradley House in Wiltshire. The Duke had succeeded to the title in 1894 on the death of his father, whose two elder brothers had died childless.

A large, athletic man, over six feet tall, the Duke, Algernon St Maur, was known affectionately by his friends as 'Anak' (the giant in the Hebrew Bible). He attended Britannia Naval College, joined the 60th Rifles and was active with the army in Canada. He was much taken with the region, and after leaving the army, spent a number of years ranching in the American West. His time of military service was succinctly summed up as 'the officer who had carried the heaviest pack and who was the most skilful steersman of a boat through dangerous water'.[211] Renowned and admired for his 'fine physique and courtly manner', the Duke was, for many, the perfect example of an English gentleman. At the coronation of King George V, 'as

Mr E. Cassel as Velázquez

the hereditary bearer of the Orb, he made a picturesque and stately figure'. And although an admirer observed that he was 'Every inch a Duke', he was 'the traditional English country squire – the man of simple tastes and homely habits, whose visits (and they were frequent) were welcome to all his tenants'.[212]

In the midst of the Marlborough House set, the politicians, financiers and plutocrats, the Duke – second of the realm – and Duchess stood apart, the perfect personification of a yesteryear of England that still appealed to so many. The Duchess, Susan Mackinnon, was from Scotland, and was also an outdoor enthusiast and intrepid explorer. The couple spent months on a camping journey across Canada, which she chronicled in a very successful book, *Impressions of a Tenderfoot during a Journey in the Far West*, in 1890. Travelling to remote areas, hunting, shooting, playing sports such as tennis and golf, the popular and amiable pair were admirably well-suited. They were equally devoted to philanthropy, and were active in the Dr Barnardo's charity for young people, both serving on the Board (the Duke was President) and as passionate fundraisers. They entertained children every year at their home.

Susan Mackinnon was a talented writer and artist, and a committed social worker. She was for thirty-five years a leader in the National Society for the Prevention of Cruelty to Children (NSPCC) and the Red Cross. Made a Dame Grand Cross of the Order of St John of Jerusalem, she also received decorations from France, Serbia and Spain for her work with the sick and wounded during the First World War.

The challenges of the Somerset title continued, as the 15th Duke was the eighth of his line to die without issue – and the title was for a time in dispute before his cousin Brigadier-General Sir Edward Hamilton Seymour became the 16th Duke. This resilience to the issues of providing a male heir has been a feature of the hardiness of the line, which still stands as one of the most ancient in the peerage. Algernon Seymour, with his strong and handsome physique and genial manner, embodied the quintessentially public-spirited gentleman devoted to his estates and to country pursuits. A traditional Tory, he took his responsibilities seriously, serving as Colonel with the First Wiltshire Volunteers, and taking on the duties of Justice of the Peace. His aversion to smoking, drinking, gambling and racing, and his appetite for public works and outdoor living, were in direct contrast to many of the late nineteenth-century trends that were apparent at the Jubilee Ball. He and the Duchess, in their historically accurate and splendid costumes, provided a vivid reminder of a Britain fast disappearing.

VI

THE AFTERMATH

F OR ALL ITS MAGNIFICENCE AND SPLENDOUR, the Diamond Jubilee marked what, in retrospect, is seen as a high mark of patriotic fervour. Indeed, there was an increasing lack of enthusiasm for the expense and effort of governing such a huge imperial spread over peoples and territory, so much so that, during the 1880s and 1890s, large numbers of chartered companies were granted what had been government powers of levying taxes and maintaining internal order. This system, combined with the collaboration with native emirs, sultans, princes and chieftains, was fine as far as it went, but was unsustainable in cases of conflict.

The start of the Boer War in 1899 in southern Africa led to a massive shock for Britain when, instead of easily overpowering the local Boer (Dutch) population, it took two and a half years and the deployment of 400,000 troops to secure a painful victory. British weakness was mocked by Germany, who had loudly supported the Boers. The Kaiser's open support of the Boers and the German settlers on the Cape led to a further deterioration of relations between Britain and Germany. Furthermore, difficulties with the United States had arisen in 1895 when President Cleveland, operating on the principle of the Monroe Doctrine (which asserted that America should be the dominant power throughout the Americas), threatened to intervene in the border dispute between Britain and Venezuela. Such political divisions were difficult to bear, as colleagues fell out depending on positions taken on these and other skirmishes.

But in 1897 painful blows to British supremacy were not top of the agenda for those elites for whom the Empire was an impregnable fortress providing its upper classes (and, increasingly, its plutocracy) with wealth and power. Stability had been a watchword among Britain's ruling classes since the revolutionary throes of continental Europe, and it formed a guiding

HH Princess Henry of Pless as Cleopatra

principle of British public and private life. The rise of the Radical movement had led to reform and widened suffrage, but even radical politicians such as Joseph Chamberlain were staunch imperialists. The accommodation of peaceful reform had been a hallmark of a stable imperial state, and the ability to embrace calibrations that widened power-sharing without ceding control was a critical characteristic and aspiration of the British governing elite.

The Diamond Jubilee arrived at a critical juncture of the nation's history. Britain was at the brink of tremendous change and, despite outward stability, was in considerable political turmoil. One powerful faction stridently argued that backing Britain meant supporting and promoting all that she stood for: a proud history of independence backed by a strong pound, favourable trading conditions with friends and close relationships with the English-speaking world. Another view – just as vehement and equally strongly held and articulated – spoke persuasively for an internationalist, global approach, underpinned by strong economic performance and trade agreements with nations around the world, especially the closest allies in Europe.

Thus the argument of preferential tariffs – led persuasively by Chamberlain – versus that of free trade was in open debate. Britain's role in the world was a subject of discussion by senior politicians of all parties as they struggled to define what the Empire represented, and what role the mother nation should play in its development. Countries such as Canada and Australia pushed for discounted trade, but such preferential treatment angered Britain's continental neighbours, who threatened a trade war. Opponents of imperial tariffs argued that Britain had thrived because of a global economy, free of impediments and restrictions, and that free trade led to prosperity for all. It is fascinating to observe that arguments foreshadowing the Brexit struggles featured well over a century ago.

But the nation was ready to celebrate, and corporations and enterprises large and small prepared to flood the market with souvenirs, while hotels and restaurants readied themselves for an invasion of Americans and other high-spending tourists. The magazines and newspapers strove to outdo one another, publishing page upon page of breathless articles – many of them lavishly illustrated – anticipating the parades, the displays, the royal processions and attendance at events … and the parties. Speculation ran rife over what the royals and socialites would wear to each event. Portentous matters about Britain's destiny were, for the moment, put to one side.

> The arrival and display of troops from all over the world - including 'Royal Canadian Mounted Police, Bengal Lancers, Hong Kong constabulary in long robes and conical hats, Houssas from West Africa and "handsome" Sikhs' – made a resplendent show, moving Edward Hamilton, Gladstone's private secretary, to note, 'If ever there was a moment at which one might feel proud of being a member of the British Empire it was now'.[213]

In its wake the Boer War, which ended in 1902, brought, however, in addition to the challenges of conflict, many questions about the defence of Empire. Disastrously, the war divided the Liberal Party – and division within the ranks was always a political danger. There were Liberals who espoused the tradition of foreign policy as articulated by party luminaries such as Richard Cobden and John Bright – Radicals who founded what we now think of as laissez-faire free trade – and a minimum of political involvement with trading partners. The challenges of managing Irish aspirations for Home Rule were a constant thorn in the side, especially as Irish Nationalist MPs attended Westminster and could hold the balance of power.

Discussions led by Chamberlain at a series of Colonial Conferences following the Diamond Jubilee exposed the divisions between those who sought a form of protectionism within a trade group (eventually to become the Commonwealth) and those who vehemently espoused the virtues of free trade and minimal government intervention and controls. The difficulties of acquiescing in the desire expressed by Canada and the colonial governments for preferential and special relations with Britain were the ensuing issues raised by continental and other trading partners. Tariff wars with Germany and other continental trading nations – many of whose populations were growing at higher rates than that of Britain – were a constant threat when preferential trading within the British Empire was mooted. Protectionism was one of the reasons for the 'Scramble for Africa', begun in the 1880s, whereby European nations and Britain fought for control – formal or informal – over sub-Saharan African territories and privileged access to the free markets.

We can observe that the trade problems as most recently manifested by the Brexit issues, and the ongoing challenges of managing relations with Northern Ireland amidst growing local opposition to partition, are current results of difficult problems already present in the nineteenth century (and before). Guests at the Jubilee Ball might have had differing approaches to the Empire and to the economic and social challenges facing the nation, but there was a uniformity in their loyalty to the Crown, and to the benefits of imperialism and growth. There were few Tories, perhaps, but there were no Irish sympathisers and no Radicals supporting abolition of the monarchy.

A further observation is the recognition of the astonishing webbed relationships of foreign and indigenous elites. Privilege and wealth led to social status. An Eton-educated Indian prince could meet on quasi-equal terms with British aristocrats; daughters and wives of business tycoons could display their riches embroidered on their silk gowns alongside diplomats and senior politicians. But, although it was a night where luxury, power and pleasure met, the Ball was not unalloyed joy. As is often the case, the appearance belied much of the reality. Discomfort was a major feature of the party: the Duke of Portland wrote of how his moustache, enhanced with yellow cotton wool to match his wig, caught fire at dinner and had to be rapidly extinguished in a glass. His wife was miserable, being 'terribly oppressed by the weight of her wig and costume; and we both determined that in future we would never, never dress up again'.[214]

And the knights of the Round Table, led by Lord and Lady Rodney (*see page 87*) as King Arthur and Queen Guinevere, wore strikingly authentic suits of armour – each of a different design, by the artist Sir Edward Burne-Jones, 'of chain mail with plate armour over it'. The great effect was enhanced by the presence of Mr Hall Walker (*see page 161*) as Merlin, bedecked in 'silken robes embroidered with magic symbols, with locks of long white hair falling from beneath a rough turban'. The knights, however, were unable to move without effort, their costumes hot, clanky and heavy.[215]

The party was planned to celebrate the success and splendour of the Empire. Newspapers and other media played their part in associating the fancy-dress pleasure with the national interest, recounting in minute detail the arrivals to the party, the outfits meticulously described, as well as the entertainments on offer. Spectators gaped and gasped at the lights, marvelled at the music, and were dazzled by the display. Photographs chronicling the event were widely circulated and published. If the objective of the party was to secure a statement of strength and solidity, it was hugely successful.

Examining this event with a more analytical lens, though, reveals a message of greater complexity. The finely woven web of connections, relations – collegiate and personal – on display was made up of a distinctly foreign or 'outsider' element. The hostess, as noted, was German (and spoke English with a slight accent), and the party was probably subsidised by friends of the Prince of Wales of foreign origin. Although the majority of the guest list was composed of British subjects, there was a formidable and significant showing of guests who were not from the traditional mainstream of elite society. This poses the question of what, in 1897, was meant by elite society. Cannadine has convincingly argued that, in the nineteenth century, the British aristocracy was in fact composed of a new elite, pointing out that 'most of the very wealthiest landed families in Victorian Britain traced their riches back no further than to the eighteenth and early nineteenth centuries'.[216]

It is also important to remember the distinctive nature of Victoria's ascent to the throne. Beginning in 1698, the Hanoverian Georges were imported to preserve the Protestant throne – George I, notoriously, did not even speak English. There were occasions when Bertie himself – a stickler for the respect he felt was his due – experienced reminders of the rather shallow roots of the British throne. When in Marienbad for a cure, he had admonished an Austrian noble for 'quite inadvertently', he pleasantly conceded, wearing the tie of the English Guards. When the nobleman asked him how long these had been the Guards' colours, and was informed that it had been 300 years, he replied that the colours had been his own family's colours '*for over seven hundred years*'.[217]

The German origins of Britain's monarchy meant that legitimacy was always an issue in Britain, even though there was no immediate threat to the dynasty. Victoria's use of her many sons and daughters to people the thrones of the continent was part of a strategy to legitimise power. She was adept at survival, as was her son. When the Prince of Wales ran out of money, he was happy to take cash from rich friends and then to introduce these friends to the highest circles. Members of the extended royal family and of the high nobility were prepared, as we have seen, to marry wealth of foreign and/or plutocratic origin. Indeed, many of the issues with which the high nobility became preoccupied had at their origin the problem – the lack – of money.

British high society was – with reluctance by some – prepared to follow the example provided by the royals of integrating into their groups the injection of money, ideas and influence provided by plutocrats, financiers, Americans and other foreigners. From India to Russia to continental Europe, members of the elite, deposed and dispossessed, often stripped of dignity and treasure, were drawn into the fold, with some catastrophic results. What is most remarkable is the ability of the British monarchy and ruling elite to survive and thrive by opening – with vigilance – the doors to individuals who brought benefit to the system. The legitimacy of status, with the monarch at the apex of the social pyramid, had to be buttressed by true power, which was always about money. Creative re-invention and adaptation are the trademarks of successful adaptation to inevitable change, and in 1897, a fancy-dress party played its part in accepting and embracing that change, while at the same time reinforcing the symbolic and manifest determination to preserve power and privilege on a global scale.

Mrs Sassoon as a Japanese lady

THE COSTUMES

The following is a detailed account of some of the principal costumes:[218]

The Prince of Wales as Grand Master of the Knights Hospitaller of Malta (Elizabethan period). Pourpoint of black épinglé velvet, richly embroidered steel and black jet tiny beads with passementerie of jet. Trunks formed of bands of black épinglé velvet embroidered steel over full bouillonne of steel grey silk. Mantle of black Sicilian silk with white Cross of Malta. Hauts-de-chausse, black silk sword belt of black velvet with steel mountings. Sword, black scabbard, steel belt with Cross of Malta in white enamel. High turreted top boots. Crispin gloves, hat and feathers with diamond Cross of Malta. Order, Riband of Order of Malta with jewelled Cross of Malta. Order of the Garter with pale blue riband round neck. Ruff.

The Duke of Connaught as a Military Commander (Elizabethan period.) Doublet of grey velvet, with slashed sleeves of same, the puffs of grey silk, beaded with steel cut beads. Trunks of grey velvet, with slashing of grey silk embroidered gold and studded with cabochons and steel. Mantle of grey velvet, with embroidered gold bands. Cuirasse of steel damascened with gorget and ruff attached. Trunk hose grey silk. High boots of grey leather turned back. Toque of black velvet, with grey puffs and grey feathers. Orders, Riband and Badge of the Garter. Crispin gloves of grey leather. Sword belt, grey velvet with steel mountings. Sword, black velvet scabbard, steel hilt and blade.

Prince Charles of Denmark as a Gentleman of the Court of Denmark.

Mr Alfred Rothschild as Henry III

The Hereditary Prince of Saxe-Coburg and Gotha as Duc Robert of Normandy, in coat of mail and casque.

Prince Christian as Earl of Lincoln (Elizabethan period). Black velvet costume lined with ermine; fawn satin tunic and trunks, the latter, as well as the sleeves, slashed with white satin. Black velvet cap, with white feathers fastened in with a jewelled ornament.

Princess Victoria of Schleswig-Holstein as a princess (Elizabethan period). Dress made of old turquoise and gold brocade. The front and all round skirt richly embroidered gold, bands of white satin pearled. The sleeves of blue brocade with crèves of white crepe pearled and studded gold. Cherusque old lace, embroidered gold. Small pearl crown headdress. Ecran. Pearl necklace.

The Grand Duke Michael of Russia in a Henry IV costume in black and gold, puffed with white satin and gold embroidered straps. The cape lined with white and trimmed with gold cord and tassels. White ruff. Black hat ornamented with gold braid; and blue silkband with Order.

The Duke of Teck as Capitaine de la Garde du Roi (1660). White cloth tunic, with blue revers trimmed with silver. White waistcoat to correspond. Cloth breeches, high boots and powdered peruke.

The Duchess of Teck as Princess Sophia, wife of the Elector of Lüneburg and Hanover. Orange-coloured velours miroir, the full skirt attached with two rows of large pearls holding the folds onto the bodice. The skirt trimmed with ermine, the décolleté bodice having large revers of ermine and a collarette of diamonds and pearls, from which hung on one side a lace cap attached to the hair. The costume was copied from a miniature at Hampton Court.

Prince Alexander of Teck as a Dragoon Guard of the Blenheim period, carried out in blue.

Mr L.V. Harcourt as Viscount Nuncham 1750

Prince Francis of Teck, the same in red.

Princess Victor of Hohenlohe-Lungenburg in Louis XV costume.

Countess Helena Gleichen as Joan of Arc, in a suit of armour.

Princess Henry of Pless (*see page 145*) as the Queen of Sheba. A costume of gold and purple gauze, the short-waisted bodice encrusted with immense turquoises set round with diamonds and other precious stones; the skirt and draperies of gold gauze embroidered to correspond, and the long gold girdle encrusted and fringed with jewels. Bird of paradise and crown. Four Black servants held her train.

The Duchess of Connaught as Ann of Austria. Robe of old ciselé velvet, havana colour, the turnback of skirt of rose colour silk velvet embroidered silver. Panel of havana colour silk velvet embroidered silver. Front of dress of white satin with embroidery of gold fleur-de-lys and beautiful bordered collar and cuffs of old guipare lace with seme of pearls. Very simple headdress. Bandeau, pearl and gold and plume Ecran of feathers in hand. Handsome jewelled necklace and earrings.

The Duke of York as George Clifford, Earl of Cumberland. Pourpoint and sleeves of Genoa velvet ciselé, with small basques, embroidered gold all over with bands of embroidery in front of pourpoint and side seams of sleeves certis of jewels. Trunks of bands of crimson velvet embroidered gold covering bouillonne of grey satin. Gorget of steel damasquine gold with ruff round. High felt hat, with brim turned up and three grey feathers, cordèliere glove fixed in front of hat, which this commander always wore and which was given him by Queen Elizabeth. Hauts-de-chausse grey silk. High boots grey suede. Crispin gloves. Mantle of Genoa velvet ciselé, embroidered with band all round, embroidered and studded with jewels. Sword belt of grey velvet with gold mounts. Gold hilted sword, grey velvet scabbard. Riband of the Garter round neck with Order.

Mrs Hope Vere as Medusa

The Duchess of York as Marguerite de Valois. Pale blue satin, embroidered all over in pearls and silver, with seven large diamond stars down the front of the skirt; the satin bodice embroidered in bows and knots in diamonds on the stomacher, and the top ornamented with large pendant pearls. Medici collar of old lace embroidered with silver; sleeves to match, and deep cuffs encrusted with pearls and diamonds; and round the waist a silver fringe studded with diamonds.

The Duke of Devonshire as Charles V of Germany, after the picture by Titian. Surcoat black velvet lined satin, sleeves puffed large at shoulders. The surcoat turned back in front with black fur and ending in fur cape scalloped, black-beaded embroidered pattern on end of surcoat. Doublet black Genoa velvet embroidered tiny jet clack beads, slightly open on chest, showing white shirt. Black silk trunks slashed with white satin. Hose black silk high above the knee. Black velvet shoes. Toque black velvet with feather. Black Chain and Order of the Golden Fleece round neck. Sword belt, black leather and silver fastenings. Sword, scabbard black leather, oxydised hilt.

The Duchess of Devonshire as Zenobia, Queen of Palmyra, wore a magnificent costume. The skirt of gold tissue was embroidered all over in a star-like design in emeralds, sapphires, diamonds and other jewels outlined with gold, the corners where it opened in front being elaborately wrought in the same jewels and gold to represent peacocks' outspread tails. This opened to show an underdress of cream crepe-de-chine, delicately embroidered in silver, gold, and pearls and sprinkled all over with diamonds. The train, which was attached to the shoulders by two slender points and was fastened at the waist with a large diamond ornament, was a green velvet of a lovely shade, and was superbly embroidered in Oriental designs introducing the lotus flower in rubies, sapphires, amethysts, emeralds and diamonds, with four borderings on contrasting grounds, separated with gold cord. The train was lined with turquoise satin. The bodice was composed of gold tissue to match the

Lady Gerard as Astarte, Goddess of the Moon

skirt, and the front was of crepe-de-chine hidden with a stomacher of real diamonds, rubies and emeralds. Jewelled belt. A gold crown incrusted with emeralds, diamonds, and rubies, with a diamond drop at each curved end and two upstanding white ostrich feathers in the middle, and round the front festoons of pearls with a large pear-shaped pearl in the centre falling on the forehead.

The Duke of Portland as Duc di Savoia. The Duke of Portland's costume was copied from the portrait of Villiers, Duke of Buckingham, in the National Gallery, and was carried out in black velvet and white satin with silver embroideries.

The Duchess of Portland as Duchessa di Savoia. Silver brocade embroidered with pearls and diamonds, train of cloth of silver lined with pale blue satin and embroidered with pearls, tiara of sapphires, diamonds, and pearls, and pearl necklace. The Duchess was accompanied by Miss Mildred Grenfell as Bianca di Piacoma, whose skirt was of a white satin embroidered with pearls, and a train of green brocaded silk.

The Earl of Rosebery as Horace Walpole. Coat (George III period) dark green velvet with large turn back cuffs of sage green silk. The buttonholes and cuffs delicately embroidered with silver. Star of the Order of the Garter worn on left breast. Long vest, sage green, embroidered with dark green flowers edged with silver. Breeches, dark green velvet. Hose, delicate sage grey hose coming high up and turned over in a roll. Order of the Garter worn on left knee, blue moiré riband of the Garter worn over the right shoulder. Sword belt and frog, blue velvet, embroidered with silver, worn underneath vest. Court sword, black velvet and gold hilted. Hair, powdered and queued with large black silk bow and riband coming round the neck and hanging in front on breast and tied. Real lace jabot and frilled cuffs. Black high-heeled shoes, scarlet heels and silver buckles.

Mr and Mrs Hall Walker as Merlin and Vivian

Earl of Latham as the Doge of Venice. Gold brocade gown and State robe embroidered with gold. Large ermine tippet. White cloth skull cap, and worn over that a gold cloth cap horned at back and embroidered with gold and jewels. Gold and jewelled waist belt. Cloth of gold shoes.

Countess Cadogan as Queen of Bohemia. A black velvet gown, the full skirt showing a panel of white satin studded with pearls and diamonds (worked at Viscountess Duncannan's school), the bodice plain, with large puffed sleeves and ruffles of lace. A large Vandyked lace collar, two rows of pearls encircling the waist. The collar and sleeves outlined with pearls; other rows festooned across the bodice. Ornaments, pearl necklace and bracelets, and pearls and diamonds in the hair.

The Countess of Dudley as Queen Esther. Persian dress of white crepe thickly embroidered in red dull gold. The skirt bordered with three lines of green embroidery studded with amethysts, turquoises, and pearls. A chasuble of solid gold tissue encrusted with jewels fell from the shoulders to the hem of the skirt. Armlets and bracelets of dead gold set with the same jewels. Head-dress, two veils, the under one white embroidered with gold, and the upper one purple, embroidered. Crown of dead gold, encrusted with precious stones, and hanging on the forehead were fifteen large drop pearls. Fan of peacock feathers, the handle set with jewels, and necklace of twelve rows of pearls.

The Countess of Derby as Duchess of Orléans. Rich blue silk stamped with purple velvet and trimmed with antique lace, edged with gold. Front and vest of gold and white brocade, the former showing bands of gold embroidery laid on horizontally. Train of brocaded velvet to match the bodice, draped down on side with pink satin, and held down here and there with diamond ornaments, coronet-shaped cap of lace sprinkled with diamonds and lappets.

Consuelo, Duchess of Manchester, née Yznaga del Valle

The Marchioness of Londonderry as the Empress Marie-Thérèse. Gown of rich cream satin, copied from a picture in South Kensington Museum, beautifully embroidered in shades of gold and pearls. Stomacher of diamonds with ropes of pearls festooned on each side and diamond brooches all along the top. Train of rich cream acanthus leaf brocade, fastened on the left shoulder with a huge diamond buckle caught at the waist with another. Necklace of pear-shaped pearls, with another diamond necklace above, and a crown studded with jewels.

Lady Helen Stewart, Lady Beatrix Fitzmaurice, Lady Beatrice Butler, Lady Alexandra Hamilton and **Miss Stirling** as Archduchesses in Waiting on Marie-Thérèse were dressed alike in stiff silver tissue, veiled with white lisse and half hoops of old-fashioned blue satin riband; large flounces of white lisse, and quaint sleeves, with frills and bows of blue riband.

Mr A.J. Balfour in a Dutch costume of 1660, black broche tunic embroidered with jet, full breeches, black silk cloak and large hat of the period.

Mr Joseph Chamberlain in a Louis XVI costume in two shades of rose-coloured corded silk.

The Right Hon. H.H. Asquith as a Roundhead. Light brown cloth jerkin with dark brown cloth sleeves and buttoned up the front. Breeches, dark brown cloth, baggy, buttoned up the side. Boots, heavy cavalier riding boots buff, coming up above the knee. Steel spurs. Large black beaver hat, narrow crowned and broad brim, scarlet feather curling over left side. Buff leathern sword belt worn over right shoulder, steel buckles. Heavy steel hilted sword. Black leather scabbard, Roundhead collar and cuffs. Walking stick.

Lady Harcourt as a lady of the Court of Henrietta Maria in maize brocade, slashed with white, over a white quilted petticoat.

The Duke of Somerset as Edward, Duke of Somerset,
Lord Protector of England

Viscount Peel as a doge in a robe of crimson velvet, with ermine cape and horned cap.

The Duchess of Sutherland as Charlotte Corday in a soft clinging gown of red crepe-de-chine, with long sleeves to the waist, finely tucked white fichu fastened with roses and muslin cap frilled with point d'Alençon, and having a red, white, and blue rosette.

The Duchess of Westminster as Queen Elizabeth of Bavaria in a white satin gown with tabbed bodice delicately embroidered in a silver collar of beautiful old lace very high at the back, slashed sleeves of satin, silver embroidery, and chiffon divided into puffs with blue.

The Countess of Warwick as Marie Antoinette in a bodice and paniers of pink- and gold-flowered brocade and gold lace studded with silver sequins and diamonds, the square-cut neck trimmed with old lace, and the chiffon sleeves divided into small puffs with gold lace sparkling with jewels; diamond rivieres were festooned across the front of the bodice. The petticoat was of white satin draped with chiffon scarves edged with gold and sequin lace. The regal train of turquoise velvet was lined with the same and enbroidered all over at equal distance with raised gold fleur-de-lys, and fastened on each of the shoulders with gold cord.

The Marchioness of Zetland as Henrietta Maria, wife of Charles I, after Van Dyck, in black and silver.

The Marchioness of Lansdowne as a lady of the Court of Marie-Thérèse in a white brocaded sacque, elaborately embroidered in gold, and under-dress worked in coloured silk and gold.

The Marquis of Lansdowne as Count Kaunitz, Minister to the Empress Marie-Thérèse, in a uniform of black velvet, elaborately embroidered in gold with orders.

The Duchess of Somerset as Jane, Queen of England, wife to King Henry the Eighth and mother to King Edward the Sixth

BIBLIOGRAPHY

Articles, Journals, Magazines, Newspapers and Websites

Walter L. Arnstein, 'Queen Victoria's Diamond Jubilee', in *The American Scholar*, Vol.66, No 4 (Autumn 1997), pp.591–97 (The Phi Beta Kappa Society).

Theodore H. Boggs, 'The British Empire and Closer Union', in *The American Political Science Review*, vol.X, November 1916, No.4, pp.635–53.

Zev Eleff, 'How New York's 19th-century Jews turned Purim into an American Party', on *The Conversation*, 23 February 2021.

Russell Harris, *Dreams of Orient & Occident* www.rvondeh.dircon.co.uk; also *Background to the Devonshire House Ball* www.rovondeh.dircon.co.uk 'in calm prose'. The work of curator Russell Harris in the preparation of the V&A exhibition of 2011 was very helpful, and his work on cataloguing the Lafayette archive invaluable.

Janice Helland, 'Rural Women and Urban Extravagance in Late Nineteenth-Century Britain', in *Rural History* (2002) 13, 2, pp.179–97 (Cambridge, UK: Cambridge University Press).

Holt, Ardern, 1879, *Fancy Dresses Described; or, What to Wear at Fancy Dress Balls*, 1st edition. London: Debenham & Freebody.

Holt, Ardern, 1880, *Fancy Dresses Described; or, What to Wear at Fancy Dress Balls*, 2nd edition. London: Debenham & Freebody.

Holt, Ardern, 1882, *Fancy Dresses Described; or, What to Wear at Fancy Dress Balls*, 3rd edition. London: Debenham & Freebody.

Holt, Ardern, 1887, *Fancy Dresses Described; or, What to Wear at Fancy Dress Balls*, 5th edition. London: Debenham & Freebody.

Holt, Ardern, 1896, *Fancy Dresses Described; or, What to Wear at Fancy Dress Balls*, 6th edition. London: Debenham & Freebody.

Holt, Ardern, 1882, *Gentleman's Fancy Dress: How to Choose It*.
London: Debenham & Freebody.

IMAGES, Journal of Jewish Art and Visual Culture, 2021.

Jenna Weissman Joselit, 'Having a Ball on Purim', in *Tablet*, 15 March 2022.

Her Majesty's Diamond Jubilee: Official Parade State of Naval Military Colonial and Auxiliary Forces June 22nd 1897 (London: J.J. Keliner & Co., 1897).

Anthony Howe, 'Towards the "hungry forties": free trade in Britain, *c*.1880–1906', in *Citizen and Community: Liberals, radicals and collective identities in the British Isles 1865–1931,* ed. Eugenio Biagini (Cambridge, UK: Cambridge University Press, 2002/1996), pp.193-218.

Ludmilla Jordanova, 'Portraiture, Biography and Public Histories', in *Transactions of the Royal Historical Society* (2022), 32, 1–4, pp.159–75 (Cambridge, UK: Cambridge University Press).

Michele Klein, 'Louis XIII, Richard I and the Duchess of Devonshire: Nineteenth century Jews in Fancy dress costume'. *IMAGES, Journal of Jewish Art and Visual Culture,* 14 (1), 2021, pp.54–81.

Liberty's Fancy-Dress: Picturesque and Fancy Dresses Including Selections From Some of the Notable Fashions in the Past History of Costumes (London: 1907).

Rebecca Mitchell, 2016, 'The Victorian Fancy Dress Ball, 1870–1900', *Fashion Theory.* https://doi.org/10.1080/1362704X.2016.1172817 (accessed 13 October 2023).

Jane Rendell, *Journal of Architectural Education* (1984–), February 2002, Vol.55, No.3, pp.136-49.

Helene Roberts, 'The Exquisite Slave: The Role of Clothes in the Making of the Victorian Woman', in *Signs*, Vol.2, No.3 (Spring 1977), pp.554–69 (The University of Chicago Press Journals).

Rothschildarchive.org

Gretchen Schneider, 'Review: The Duchess of Devonshire's Ball by Sophia Murphy' in *Dance Chronicle*, Vol.10, No.2 (1987), pp. 236–41.

Sikhmuseum.org.uk

Martin Spies, 'Late Victorian aristocrats and the racial other: the Devonshire House ball of 1897', in *Race & Class*, Institute of Race Relations, Vol.57(4), pp.95–103.

The Queen's London: A Pictorial and Descriptive Record of the Great Metropolis in the Year of Her Majesty's Diamond Jubilee (London: Cassell, 1897).

Apollo, Country Life, 1914; *Hull Daily Mail; The Illustrated London News*, Vol. CXI. July–December 1897; *The Lady's Realm; New York Herald; New York Times; Pall Mall Gazette; Queen; Tablet; The Conversation; The Times; Westminster Gazette*

Biography, Autobiography, Published Diaries & Letters

Jane Abdy and Charlotte Gere, *The Souls* (London: Sidgwick & Jackson, 1984).

R.J.Q Adams, *The Last Grandee* (London: John Murray, 2007).

Sushila Anand, *Daisy: The Life and Loves of the Countess of Warwick* (London: Piatkus, 2008).

Margot Asquith, *Margot Asquith: An Autobiography* (London: Hutchinson & Co., 1920).

E.A.M. Asquith, *More Memories* (London: Cassell and Company, 1933).

E.A.M. Asquith, *Off the Record* (London: Frederick Muller, 1943).

Consuelo Vanderbilt Balsan, *The Glitter and the Gold* (London: Hodder & Stoughton, 2012/1953).

Peter Bance, *The Duleep Singhs: The Photograph Album of Queen Victoria's Maharajah* (Gloucestershire, UK: Sutton, 2004).

Maurice Baring, *The Puppet Show of Memory* (Boston: Little, Brown & Co., 1923).

E.F. Benson, *As We Were: A Victorian Peep-Show* (London: Longmans, 1930).

Michael Bentley, *Lord Salisbury's World: Conservative Environments in Late-Victorian Britain* (Cambridge, UK: Cambridge University Press, 2007/2001).

Maurice V. Brett, ed., *Journals and Letters of Reginald Viscount Esher*, Vol.I, 1870–1903.

Jamie H. Cockfield, *White Crow: The Life and Times of the Grand Duke Nicholas Mikhailovich Romanov, 1859–1919* (London and Westport, CT: Praeger, 2002).

S. Collier, ed., *Journals of Mary, Lady Monkswell, 1895–1909.*

Damian Collins, *Charmed Life: The Phenomenal World of Philip Sassoon* (London: William Collins, 2017/2016).

Mrs George Cornwallis West, *The Reminiscences of Lady Randolph Churchill* (London: Edward Arnold, 1908).

Leonard Cottrell, *Madame Tussaud* (London: Evans, 1951).

Anne de Courcy, *Circe: the Life of Edith, Marchioness of Londonderry* (London: Sinclair-Stevenson, 1992).

Anne de Courcy, *The Viceroy's Daughters: the Lives of the Curzon Sisters* (London: Weidenfeld & Nicolson, 2000).

Devonshire House Fancy Dress Ball July 2nd 1897: A Collection of Portraits in Costume of Some of the Guests (London: privately printed for the Committee, 1899).

David Duff, *Hessian Tapestry* (London: Frederick Muller, 1967).

Max Egremont, *Balfour: A Life of Arthur James Balfour* (London: Phoenix, 1998/1980).

T.H.S. Escott, *Social Transformations of the Victorian Age: A Survey of Court and Country* (London: Seeley & Co., 1897).

T.H.S. Escott, *Society in the New Reign* (London: T. Fisher Unwin, 1904).

Lady Augusta Fane, *Chit-Chat* (London: Thornton Butterworth, 1926).

Niall Ferguson, *The House of Rothschild: The World's Banker 1849–1999* (London: Penguin, 2000/1999).

Amitav Ghosh, *'Smoke and Ashes', Opium's Hidden Histories* (London: John Murray, 2024).

Simon Heffer, *Power and Place: the Political Consequences of Edward VII* (London: Orion, 1999).

Bernard Holland, *The Life of Spencer Compton, Eighth Duke of Devonshire*, 2 vols (London: Longmans, Green and Co., 1911).

Patrick Jackson, *Harcourt & Son: A Political Biography of Sir William Court, 1827–1904* (New Jersey: Fairleigh Dickinson University Press, 2004).

Stanley Jackson, *The Sassoons* (London: Heinemann, 1968).

Roy Jenkins, *Sir Charles Dilke, a Victorian Tragedy* (London: Collins, 1959).

Roy Jenkins, *Gladstone* (London: Pan, 2002/1995).

Elisabeth Kehoe, *Fortune's Daughters: The Extravagant Lives of the Jerome Sisters, Jennie Churchill, Clara Frewen and Leonie Leslie* (London: Atlantic, 2004).

Simon Kerry, *Lansdowne: The Last Great Whig* (London: Unicorn, 2017).

James Lees-Milne, *The Enigmatic Edwardian: The Life of Reginald 2nd Viscount Esher* (London: Sidgwick & Jackson, 1988/1986).

Natalie Livingstone, *The Women of Rothschild: The Untold Story of the World's Most Famous Dynasty* (London: John Murray, 2022/2021).

Norman and Jeanne MacKenzie, eds, *The Diary of Beatrice Webb, Volume Two 1892–1905: 'All the Good Things of Life'* (London: Virago, with the LSE, 1983).

Amanda Mackenzie Stuart, *Consuelo & Alva: The Story of a Mother and a Daughter in the Gilded Age* (London: HarperCollins, 2005).

The Duke of Manchester, *My Candid Recollections* (London: Grayson & Grayson, 1932).

Peter T. Marsh, *Joseph Chamberlain: Entrepreneur in Politics* (New Haven, CT and London: Yale University Press, 1994).

Grand Duke Michael Michaelowitch, *Never Say Die* (London: Collier & Co., 1908).

Sophia Murphy, *The Duchess of Devonshire's Ball* (London: Sidgwick & Jackson, 1984).

Ralph Neville, ed., *The Reminiscences of Lady Dorothy Nevill* (London: Edward Arnold, 1906).

Gregory D. Phillips, *The Diehards: Aristocratic Society and Politics in Edwardian England* (Cambridge, MA.: Harvard University Press, 1979).

Pamela Pilbeam, *Madame Tussaud and the History of Waxworks* (London and New York: Hambledon and London, 2003).

Paul Poiret, *My First Fifty Years*, trans. Stephen Haden Guest (London: Victor Gollancz, 1931).

The Duke of Portland, *Men, Women and Things* (London: Faber & Faber, 1937).

Eileen Quelch, *Perfect Darling: Life and Times of George Cornwallis-West* (London: Cecil Woolf, 1972).

Michaela Reid, *Ask Sir James* (London: Hodder & Stoughton, 1987).

Jane Ridley, *Bertie: A Life of Edward VII* (London: Chatto & Windus, 2012).

Edith Saunders, *The Age of Worth: Couturier to the Empress Eugenie* (London: Longmans, 1954).

Robert and Elizabeth Shackleton, *Four on a Tour in England* (New York: Hearst's International Library Co., Inc., 1914).

Peter Stansky: *Sassoon: The Worlds of Philip and Sybil* (New Haven, CT: Yale University Press, 2012).

Raleigh Trevelyan, *Grand Dukes and Diamonds: The Wernhers of Luton Hoo* (London: Secker & Warburg, 1991).

Diane Urquhart, *The Ladies of Londonderry: Women and Political Patronage* (London: I.B. Tauris, 2007).

Henry Vane, *Affair of State: A Biography of the 8th Duke and Duchess of Devonshire*
(London: Peter Owen, 2004).

Frances Countess of Warwick (Daisy), *Afterthoughts*
(London: Cassell and Company, Ltd., 1931).

Mrs. Hwfa Williams, *It Was Such Fun* (London: Hutchinson, 1935).

General

Alison Adburgham, *Shops and Shopping 1800–1914: Where, and In What Manner The Well-Dressed Englishwoman Bought Her Clothes* (London: George Allen and Unwin, 1981/1964).

David Cannadine, *Aspects of Aristocracy: Grandeur and Decline in Modern Britain*
(London and New Haven, CT: Yale University Press, 1994).

David Cannadine, *The Decline and Fall of the British Aristocracy*
(New Haven, CT and London: Yale University Press, 1992/1990).

David Cannadine, *Lords and Landlords. The Aristocracy and the Towns, 1774–1967*
(Leicester: Leicester University Press, 1980).

Terry Castle, *Masquerade and Civilisation: The Carnivalesque in Eighteenth-Century English Culture and Fiction* (Stanford, CA.: Stanford University Press, 1986).

Christopher Clark, *Revolutionary Spring: Fighting for a New World 1848–1849*
(UK: Allen Lane, 2023).

Cynthia Cooper, *Magnificent Entertainments: Fancy Dress Balls of Canada's Governors General 1876–1898* (New Brunswick: Goose Lane Editions, 1997).

Quentin Crewe, *The Frontiers of Privilege* (London: Collins, 1961).

J. Mordaunt Crook, *The Rise of the Nouveaux Riches* (London: John Murray, 1999).

Diana de Marley, *The History of Haute Couture* (London: Batsford, 1980).

Diana de Marley, *Worth: Father of Haute Couture* (London: Elm Tree Books, 1980).

Nancy W. Ellenberger, *Balfour's World: Aristocracy and Political Culture at the Fin de Siècle*
(Woodbridge, Suffolk: The Boydell Press, 2015).

David Feldman, *Englishmen and Jews: Social Relations and Political Culture 1840–1914*
(New Haven, CT and London: Yale University Press, 1994).

Geoffrey Finlayson, *Citizen, State, and Social Welfare in Britain 1830–1990*
(Oxford: Clarendon, 1994).

Judith Flanders, *Consuming Passions: Leisure and Pleasure in Victorian Britain* (London: HarperPress, 2006).

Peter Frankopan, *The Earth Transformed: An Untold History* (London: Bloomsbury, 2023).

Simon Heffer: *High Minds: The Victorians and the Birth Of Modern Britain* (London: Windmill, 2014/2013).

Simon Heffer, *The Age of Decadence: Britain 1880 to 1914* (London: Windmill Books, 2018/2017).

Erica E. Hirschler with Caroline Corbeau-Parsons, James Finch, and Pamela A. Parmal: *Sargent and Fashion* (Boston, MA: Max Publications, Museum of Fine Arts, 2023).

Robert Holland, *Blue-Water Empire: The British in the Mediterranean since 1800* (London: Allen Lane, 2012).

Ardern Holt, *Fancy Dresses Described; or What to Wear at Fancy Balls*, 5th edn (London: Debenham & Freebody, 1887).

Eric Homberger, *Mrs Astor's New York: Money and Social Power in a Gilded Age* (New Haven, CT and London: Yale University Press, 2002).

Pamela Horn, *Pleasures & Pastimes in Victorian Britain* (Gloucestershire, UK: Amberley, 2001/1999).

Anthea Jarvis, *Fancy Dress* (Aylesbury, Bucks: Shire Publications, 1894).

Mark Knowles, *The Wicked Waltz and Other Scandalous Dances* (Jefferson, NC, and London: McFarland & Company, Inc., 2009).

Peter Mandler, *History and National Life* (London: Profile Books, 2002).

Peter Mandler, *The Fall and Rise of the Stately Home* (New York and London: Yale University Press, 1997).

Geoffrey C. Munn, *Tiaras: A History of Splendour* (Suffolk, UK: ACC Art Books 2023/2001).

Allan Nevins, *Thirty Years of American Diplomacy* (New York and London: Harper, 1930).

Harold Perkin, *The Rise of Professional Society: England Since 1880* (London and New York: Routledge, 1989).

Terence Pepper, Intro. by Hugo Vickers, *High Society: Photographs 1897–1914* (London: National Portrait Gallery Publications, 1998).

G.D. Phillips, *The Diehards: Aristocratic Society and Politics in Edwardian England*
(Cambridge, MA: Harvard University Press, 1979).

John Pick, *The West End: Mismanagement and Snobbery* (London: City Arts Series, 1983)

Harold Pollins, *Economic History of the Jews in England*
(Rutherford, NJ: Fairleigh Dickinson University Press, 1982).

Andrea Geddes Poole, *Stewards of the Nation's Art: Contested Cultural Authority 1890–1939*
(Toronto: University of Toronto Press, 2010),

Frank Prochaska, *Royal Bounty: The Making of a Welfare Monarchy*
(New Haven and London: Yale University Press, 1995),

Charlotte Ribeyrol, Matthew Winterbottom and Madeline Hewitson, eds,
Colour Revolution: Victorian Art, Fashion, & Design
(Oxford: Ashmolean Museum, University of Oxford, 2023),

W.D. Rubinstein, *Capitalism, Culture, and Decline in Britain 1750–1990*
(London and New York: Routledge, 1994/1993),

W.D. Rubinstein, *Men of Property: The Very Wealthy in Britain Since the Industrial
Revolution* (Brighton: Edward Everett Root, 2016/2006/1981),

G.R. Searle, *A New England: Peace and War 1886–1918* (Oxford: Clarendon, 2004),

Anne Somerset, *Unnatural Murder: Poison at the Court of James I*
(London: Weidenfeld & Nicolson, 1997),

Kurt von Stutterheim, *The Press in England*, trans. W.H. Johnson
(London: George Allen & Unwin Ltd., 1934),

F.M.L. Thompson, *English Landed Society in the Nineteenth Century*
(Oxford: Routledge, 2007/1963),

F.M.L. Thompson, *The Rise of Respectable Society: A Social History of Victorian Britain
1830–1900* (London: Fontana, 1988),

Angus Trumble and Andrea Wolk Rager, eds, *Edwardian Opulence: British Art at the Dawn
of the Twentieth Century* (New Haven, CT and London: Yale University Press, 2013)

Alwyn Turner, *Little Englanders: Britain in the Edwardian Era*
(London: Profile Books Ltd., 2024)

Hannah Rose Woods, *Rule, Nostalgia: A Backwards History of Britain*
(London: W.H. Allen, 2023/2022)

ENDNOTES

I: INTRODUCTION

[1] *Western Gazette*, 9 July 1897.

[2] Cornwallis-West, *Reminiscences*, p.304. Full details of publications cited are given in the Bibliography.

II: HISTORICAL BACKGROUND

[3] Harold Perkin, *The Rise of Professional Society*, p.31.

[4] *Ibid.*, p.33.

[5] Peter Frankopan, *The Earth Transformed*, p.458.

[6] *Blackburn Standard*, 15 April 1899.

[7] Mrs H.H. Longman, *Northern, Scot and Moray & Nairn Express*, 14 Oct. 1905.

[8] Simon Heffer, *High Minds*, p.110.

[9] See W. Rubinstein, *Capitalism, Culture, and Decline in Britain*, p.140.

[10] *Ibid.*, pp.35–6.

[11] C.H. Rolph, *London Particulars*, p.71; cited by John Pick, *The West End: Mismanagement and Snobbery*, p.99.

[12] *Isle of Wight County Press and South of England Reporter*, 26 Jan. 1901, in Alwyn Turner, *Little Englanders*, p.7.

[13] Barbara Drake and Margaret I. Cole, eds, *Our Partnership by Beatrice Webb*; cited by F.M.L. Thompson, *English Landed Society*, p.300.

[14] Frances Countess of Warwick (Daisy), *Afterthoughts*, pp.46–7.

[15] Drake and Cole, *op. cit.*

[16] Thompson, *op. cit.*, p.300.

[17] Calculated by W.R. Rubinstein and cited in n.33 by Michael Bentley, *Lord Salisbury's World*, p.108.

[18] Bentley, *ibid.*

[19] David Cannadine, *The Decline and Fall of the British Aristocracy*, p.346.

[20] *Ibid.*

[21] Cited by Jane Ridley, *Bertie*, p.10. This is an excellent and comprehensive study of Albert Edward's life.

[22] Warwick, *op. cit.*, p.2.

[23] James Lees-Milne, *The Enigmatic Edwardian: The Life of Reginald 2nd Viscount Esher*, p.105.

24 Reginald Brett to Milly Sutherland, 18 June 1897, in Lees-Milne, *ibid.*, p.105.

25 Ridley, *op. cit.*, pp.320–21.

26 Miles Taylor, 'The 1848 Revolutions and the British Empire', *Past & Present* 166/I. (2000), pp.146–80, in Christopher Clark, *Revolutionary Spring*, p.339.

27 See Clark, *ibid.,* for a discussion and analysis of revolutionary movements in continental Europe.

28 All quotations in this paragraph from Daniel Feldman, *Englishmen and Jews*, p.263.

29 L. Putterman and D. Weil, 'Post-1500 Population Flows and the Long-Run Determinants of Economic Growth and Inequality', *Quarterly Journal of Economics* 125 (2010), 1627–82, in Peter Frankopan, *op. cit.*, p.458. See Frankopan for a fuller discussion of these enormous shifts and their global implications.

30 With a nod to Mick Herron, *Slough House*.

31 *Illustrated London News*, 18 Sept. 1897.

32 The Duchess of Devonshire was known as both 'Louise' and 'Louisa'; for simplicity, she will be referred to as 'Louise' in the text.

33 F.M.L. Thompson, *The Rise of Respectable Society*, p.106.

34 *Ibid.*

35 *Ibid.*, p.43.

36 *Ibid.*

37 *Ibid.*

38 *Ibid.*, p.153.

39 *Ibid.*, p.154.

40 W.D. Rubinstein, *Men of Property*, p.239.

41 *Ibid.*, p.240.

42 *Ibid.*, pp.241–42.

43i *Illustrated London News*, 3 July 1897.

43ii *Ibid.*

44 *Ibid.*

45 *Ibid.* 5 June 1897.

46 Warwick, *op. cit.,* p.38.

47 Peter T. Marsh, *Joseph Chamberlain: Entrepreneur in Politics*, p.532.

48 Cited by Cannadine, *Decline and Fall*, *op. cit.*, p.328. See chapters 7, 'The "Corruption" of Public Life', and 8, 'The Dilution of Select Society', for a seminal study on changes in high society from the 1880s.

49 See The Royal Mint:
https://www.royalmint.com/stories/collect/queen-victorias-pioneering-jubilees/ (accessed 29 Dec. 2023).

III: POWER AND PURPOSE

50 *Illustrated London News*, 10 July 1897.

51 Anne Somerset, *Unnatural Murder: Poison at the Court of James I*, p.6.

52 See the excellent *Masquerade and Civilization* by Terry Castle, in particular 'The Masquerade and Eighteenth-Century England'.

53 *Ibid*.

54 *Ibid*., p.341.

55 *The Illustrated Sporting and Dramatic News*, 26 June 1897.

56 Henry Vane, *Affair of State*, p.115.

57 Alison Adburgham, *Shops and Shopping, 1800–1914: Where, and in What Manner The Well-dressed Englishwoman Bought her Clothes*, p.33.

58 *Ibid*., p.35.

59 *Ibid*., p.37.

60 Pamela Horn, *Pleasures & Pastimes of Victorian Britain*, p.17.

61 Julian Fellowes, interview in *Entertainment Weekly*, 5 April 2002. Fellowes won the Oscar for best screenwriter for *Gosford Park*.

62 *Edinburgh Evening News*, 12 July 1897.

63 Adburgham, *op. cit.*

64 *The Stage*, 8 July 1897.

IV: THE EXTRAVAGANZA

65 *The Times*, 3 July 1897.

66 *Country Life*, 22 August 1914, Vol.XXXVI No.920.

67 Gail Hamilton (Mary Abigail Dodge), *Women's Worth and Worthlessness*; cited by Erica E. Hirshler and James Finch, 'Curator's Preface', *Sargent and Fashion*, p.10.

68 Hirshler and Finch, *Ibid*., p.11.

69 *Ibid*., p.59.

70 Warwick, *op. cit.*, p.161.

71 See Mark Knowles, *The Wicked Waltz and Other Scandalous Dances*, ch.3; in particular pp.30–34.

72 Almack's, the 'seventh heaven of the fashionable world', was a private club devoted at various junctures to gambling, socialising and, finally, dancing for the most exclusive members of society. At its peak, having an Almack's voucher – possession of which was decided by a committee of society *grandes dames* –

guaranteed a season of High Society, prized by all. By the 1850s it was in decline, and ended its life in 1863. The club had, however, played a major role in both legitimising and glamorising dancing in town for the upper classes.

73 *Hull Daily Mail*, 6 July 1897.

74 Sophia Murphy, *The Duchess of Devonshire's Ball*, p.72.

75 'The Democratic world', *Reynold's Newspaper*, 24 June 1894, 3, in Peter Mandler, *The Fall and Rise of the Stately Home*, p.165.

76 Lafayette continues as a successful photography firm. See the website for the history: https://www.lafayettephotography.com (last accessed 14 Nov. 2023).

77 This remarkable painting portrays Madame Pierre Gautreau in a black dress shockingly cut so low that it reveals her shoulders and a great deal of her bust.

78 Simon Heffer, *The Age of Decadence*, p.26. See pp.25–7 for a succinct overview of Sargent's impact. Also Hirshler and Finch, *op. cit.*

79 See Simon Kerry, *Lansdowne: The Last Great Whig*, p.125.

80 Michael Bentley, *Lord Salisbury's World*, p.76.

81 Vane, *op. cit.*, p.12.

V: THE PLAYERS

82 *Luton Times and Advertiser*, 9 July 1897.

83 I am grateful to the biographical information on Louise's early life provided by Henry Vane in *Affair of State*.

84 The grounds at Tandragee are now home to the Northern Ireland Tayto crisp factory.

85 Cited by Vane, *op. cit.*, p.20.

86 *Ibid.*, p.16.

87 *Hartlepool Northern Daily Mail*, 24 March 1890.

88 *Empire News & The Empire*, 23 March 1890.

89 [Bradford MSS, 8 Aug. 1875], *Disraeli*, p 320.

90 *Ibid.*, p.178.

91 *Ibid.*

92 Bernard Holland, *The Life of Spencer Compton, Eighth Duke of Devonshire*, vol.II, p.211.

93 Warwick, *op. cit.*, pp.76–7.

94 Mandler, *op. cit.*, pp. 213–14.

95 He will continue to be referred to as 'Hartington'.

96 Mrs George Cornwallis West, *The Reminiscences of Lady Randolph Churchill*, p.133.

97 Thompson, *Respectable Society*, *op. cit.*, p.267.

98 See the excellent 'The Landowner as Millionaire: The Finances of the Duke of Devonshire', pp.165–83 in David Cannadine, *Aspects of Aristocracy: Grandeur and Decline in Modern Britain*.

99 Lady Augusta Fane, *Chit-Chat*, p.108.

100 *Ibid.*, p.107.

101 *Ibid.*

102 See Cannadine, 'The Landowner as Millionaire: The Finances of the Dukes of Devonshire', in *Aspects of Aristocracy*, *op. cit.*, pp.165–83.

103 Fane, *op. cit.*, p.193.

104 Cited by Max Egremont, *Balfour: A Life of Arthur James Balfour*, p.114.

105 Lady Blanche Balfour's influence could be harsh: she set impossibly high standards for some of her children, who led miserable and undistinguished lives. Cecil gambled and forged a cheque in Arthur's name and had to flee to Australia, where he was killed falling from a horse; Eustace made an unhappy marriage and died an alcoholic; sister Alice became Arthur's devoted yet unfulfilled and unhappy housekeeper. See Egremont, *op. cit.*, p.17.

106 *Ibid.*, p.20.

107 Peter T. Marsh, *Joseph Chamberlain: Entrepreneur in Politics*, p.5.

108 *Ibid.*, p.8.

109 The Duke of Portland, *Men, Women and Things*, p.160.

110 See Egremont, *op. cit.*

111 Cornwallis-West, *op. cit.*, pp.154–55.

112 Perkin, op. cit., p.64.

113 Cited by Theodore H. Boggs, 'The British Empire and Closer Union', in *The American Political Science Review*, pp.639–40.

114 *Dundee Evening Telegraph*, 18 Oct. 1893.

115 Cited by BBC News, https://www.bbc.co.uk/news (accessed 22 Jan. 2024).

116 *Banbury Advertiser*, 8 July 1897.

117 My thanks to Michael Bentley for this pithiness: see *Lord Salisbury's World*, p.66.

118 Thompson, *op. cit.*, p.107.

119 Fane, *op. cit.*, p.201.

120 Mrs Hwfa Williams, *It Was Such Fun*, p.161.

121 Cornwallis-West, *op. cit.*, p.301.

122 *Ibid.*

123 *Ibid.*, p.302.

124 *Ibid.*

125 *Ibid.*, p.303.

126 *Ibid.*

127 *Ibid.*

128 *Ibid.*, p.304.

129 *Ibid.*

130 See the excellent Ridley, *op. cit.*, pp.263–329.

131 Williams, *op. cit.*, p.75.

132 *Ibid.*, pp.75–6.

133 *Ibid.*, pp.76-7.

134 *Ibid.*

135 Eileen Quelch, *Perfect Darling*, p.78.

136 The nickname was an abbreviation of his courtesy title Earl of Sunderland – not an allusion to his character, which was notoriously dour.

137 Consuelo Vanderbilt Balsan, *The Glitter and the Gold*, p.61.

138 *Ibid.*, pp.102–103.

139 Amanda Mackenzie Stuart's double biography, of Consuelo and her mother Alva, *Consuelo & Alva: The Story of a Mother and a Daughter in the Gilded Age*, provides more measured detail on both lives.

140 Fane, *op. cit*, p.101.

141 *Ibid.*, pp.101, 102.

142 Warwick, *op. cit.*, pp.48–49.

143 Sophia Murphy, *The Duchess of Devonshire's Ball*, p.72.

144 *Horsfield and Bishopston Record and Montepelier & District Free Press*, 25 Dec. 1897.

145 Obituary, 7 May 1892, *New York Herald*.

146 V&A website: collection.vam.ac.uk (accessed 27 Feb. 2024).

147 The Duke of Manchester, *My Candid Recollections*, p.56.

148 See Cannadine, *Decline and Fall*, *op. cit.*, p.398.

149 V&A website: collections.vam.ac.uk (accessed 27 Feb. 2024).

150 Vane, *op. cit.*, p.92.

151 H. Pollins, *Economic History of Jews in England*, p.131. See, too, Feldman, *op. cit.*

152 See the excellent Simon Heffer, *High Minds*, pp.252–63, for a discursive analysis of how Jews became, slowly, accepted into Parliament. A second landmark achievement occurred when Bertie's great friend Nathaniel de Rothschild became the first Jewish peer in 1885.

153 Cited by Perkin, *op. cit.*, p.65.

154 Thompson, *English Landed Society*, *op. cit.*, p.302.

155 *Ibid.*, p.301.

156 Cited by J. Mordaunt Crook, *The Rise of the Nouveaux Riches*, p.243.

157 *Westminster Gazette*, 24 Oct. 1893.

158 G.E.C., *The Complete Peerage*, V, App. C; Cited by Thompson, *English Landed Society*, *op. cit.*, p.307.

159 I am grateful to David Feldman for his work on this: see, in particular, *Englishmen and Jews*, *op. cit.*, pp.78–82.

160 J. Mordaunt Crook, *op. cit.*, p.154.

161 See *Ibid.*, p.157.

162 Fane, *op. cit.*, p.282.

163 In Niall Ferguson, *The House of Rothschild*, p.249.

164 *Ibid.*

165 Ridley, *op. cit.*, p.269.

166 In Ferguson, *op. cit.*, p.251.

167 See 'Events of 1901' in the National Archives: https://www.nationalarchives.gov.uk (accessed 29 Nov. 2023).

168 See Ridley, *op. cit.*, pp.268-69.

169 *Ibid.*, p.269.

170 See Heffer, *The Age of Decadence*, *op. cit.*, p.95.

171 With thanks to the work of Natalie Livingstone, *The Women of Rothschild: The Untold Story of the World's Most Famous Dynasty*, p.189.

172 Warwick, *op. cit.*, p.40.

173 Mordaunt Crook, *op. cit.*, p.156.

174 *Ibid.*

175 *Ibid.*

176 See Jane Ridley discussing Cecil Roth's views: that the social prominence of Bertie's rich Jewish pals fuelled anti-Semitism. Cecil Roth, 'The Court Jews of Edwardian England', *Jewish Social Studies*, vol.5, 1943, pp.355–66, cited by Ridley, *op. cit.*, p.271.

177 Cited by Feldman, *op. cit.*, p.81.

178 *Ibid.*, p.268.

179 *Ibid.*, p.271.

180 *Ibid.*, p.273.

181 Cited by Eric Homberger, *Mrs Astor's New York*, p.175.

182 Williams, *op. cit.*, p.91.

183 1875; cited by Vane, *op. cit.*, p.115.

184 Cited by Vane, *op. cit.*, p.167.

185 See Michele Klein, 'Louis XIII, Richard I, and the Duchess of Devonshire: Nineteenth-Century Jews in Fancy Dress Costume', *IMAGES, Journal of Jewish Art and Visual Culture.*

186 Jenna Weissman Joselit, 'Having a Ball on Purim' in *Tablet,* 15 March 2022.

187 *Ibid.*

188 *Ibid.*

189 Williams, *op. cit.*, p.77.

190 I am grateful to the work of Damian Collins on Sassoon family history. See *Charmed Life.*

191 Cited by Damian Collins, *Charmed Life*, pp.3–4.

192 Amitav Ghosh, *Smoke and Ashes*, p.154.

193 See Ghosh, *op. cit.*, pp.154–58.

194 Collins, *op. cit.*, p.7.

195 Simon Heffer, *Power and Place*, pp.67–8. See pp.66–8 for more on the Prince's growing interest in honours, as a means to reward friends for favours and financial assistance.

196 Stanley Jackson, *The Sassoons*, p.71.

197 Cited by Philip Stansky, *Sassoon: The Worlds of Philip and Sybil*, p.15.

198 Cited by Mordaunt Crook, *op. cit.*, p.160.

199 Peter Bance, *The Duleep Singhs*, p.47.

200 Sikhmuseum.org.uk (accessed 5 March 2024).

201 Grand Duke Michael Michaelowitch, *Never Say Die*, p.vii.

202 Perceval Gibbon, 'What Ails Russia', in *McClure*, 24 Nov. 1905, p.615; cited by Jamie H. Cockfield, *White Crow*, p.3.

203 Cockfield, *ibid.*, p.17. See chapter 1 for background on Mikhail and his family.

204 *Northern Times and the Weekly Journal for Sutherland and North*, 26 May 1904.

[205] George's father, Prince Louis, had had to resign as First Sea Lord because of his German origins, after the start of the First World War. He owed money in Russia, and his property in Germany could not be accessed – he claimed that the most that he could afford for George was £350 per annum. See Raleigh Trevelyan, *Grand Dukes and Diamonds*, p.273. George's siblings were Princess Alice (mother of Prince Philip, Duke of Edinburgh), the Queen of Sweden, and Louis Battenberg, 1st Earl Mountbatten of Burma: the family anglicised their name to Mountbatten in 1917 when they gave up their German (enemy) titles and were granted British ones. Prince George was granted the title of Earl of Medina and then became 2nd Marquess of Milford Haven upon his father's death in 1921.

[206] Trevelyan, *op. cit.*, p.282.

[207] *Ibid.*

[208] *Ibid.*, p.286.

[209] *Ibid.*, p.310.

[210] Philip Mountbatten married Princess Elizabeth Windsor, who succeeded to the throne in 1952 as Elizabeth II.

[211] 27 Oct. 1923, *Wiltshire Times and Trowbridge Advertiser.*

[212] *Ibid.*

VI: THE AFTERMATH

[213] Anne Somerset, *Queen Victoria and her Prime Minister*, p.492.

[214] Portland, *op. cit.*, p.160.

[215] I am grateful for the details provided by the work of Lady Sophia Topley, in Sophia Murphy, *The Duchess of Devonshire's Ball*, p.151.

[216] Cannadine, *Aspects of Aristocracy, op. cit.*, pp.34–5.

[217] Manchester, *op. cit.*, p.59.

THE COSTUMES

[218] The compilation for the costume descriptions is sourced as follows:
Daily Graphic 10 July 1897; *Dundee Daily Telegraph* 3 July 1897;
Morning Post 3 July 1897; and *The Times* 3 July 1897.

Mrs Ronalds as Euterpe

ACKNOWLEDGEMENTS

I AM GRATEFUL TO THE MANY HISTORIANS, researchers, journalists, curators and writers whose work has proved so essential to this book. The broad stretch of historical background, combined with the detailed studies of individual lives, made the reliance on high-quality sources a hugely important plank of this work. I was so fortunate in having access to such a richness of material.

Research by Lady Sophia Topley (as Sophia Murphy) on the Devonshire House Jubilee Ball, published forty years ago, was extremely useful, and I am grateful to her for discussing it with me, and for her encouragement. Curator Russell Harris has made a splendid job of curating the Lafayette Archive of photographs of the Ball, accompanied by his meticulous research. Matt Loughrey has furthered the exciting technology of colourising original black and white photographs, which has provided us with a brilliant recreation of the event.

Curators and archivists at the Victoria & Albert Museum Art Library, at the National Portrait Gallery, the British Library, the London Library and at Chatsworth were extremely helpful, as were my always impressive colleagues at the Institute of Historical Research and the School of Advanced Studies at the University of London. Thank you.

At Unicorn Publishing I owe deepest thanks to Lucy Duckworth, who has championed this project since its inception. Elisabeth Ingles was a wonderfully thorough and encouraging editor, and I am grateful to Anna Hopwood and Felicity Price-Smith for the marvellous work with pictures and design. Thank you to Ramona Lamport for proofreading and to Marian Aird for the Index. Antonia Reeves did a splendid job on publicity, which is greatly appreciated.

Family and friends have provided invaluable support, for which I am so grateful. As ever, my most profound thanks and deepest love go to Conor, and my gratitude and love to Cassian. This book is dedicated to the lights of my heart: Emily and Alice.

INDEX